D1605923

The Truth So Far...

A detective's journey to reunite with her birth family

Jennifer Dyan Ghoston

ISBN:-10:1518609104
ISBN-13:978-1518609107

Edited by: John Harten
Cover design: Rashina Bhula
Author photo on back cover: Shirley Colvin

DEDICATION

This book is dedicated to my Ghoston and Upshaw family. You both ultimately allowed for the evidence of nurture and nature from two different families being counterparts that fit, complete or complement one another.

With love, Jennifer...aka Bonnie

CONTENTS

ACKNOWLEDGMENTS

I want to thank so many people who made this book possible. First, my family and friends have been such an inspiration. I thank all of you. I thank my community of adoptees, adoptive and birth parents who have given their precious time over the past five years to share information that helped me better process my experience. I thank my police family who imparted much wisdom over the years and kept me safe throughout my career. I particularly want to thank Griselda Walls for her decades of friendship and being available to help me at a moment's notice. I thank Gail Tubbs for all those late night conversations over the phone to keep me focused on my vision of adding a positive contribution to the adoption community. I deeply appreciate Ricky Boone for listening to my countless thoughts on this subject day after day when I first considered a birth family reunion. I thank Johnnie Minter-Edwards for being right by my side during the search for my birth family. I thank Vandella Hancock for her daily well-being checks during my good grind in the final hours to complete this book. I thank my writing coach, Nina Elaine Borum and group accountability partner, Angela J. Ford who both worked with me for months to accomplish this goal. Last, but certainly not least, I want to thank our Creator for being my constant Source and supply.

INTRODUCTION

The issue of adoption is an emotionally charged one for many adoptees and it was no different for me. So, as with nearly anything I experience, I'd like to think that I either consciously or subconsciously allowed my chosen career path to play a major role in processing this thing called life on a deeply personal level. I learned during times of reflection in the preparation of this book, that my line of work and main source of income actually readied me for the most emotional investigation of all; the search for original family members.

After spending nearly 25 years in law enforcement and over thirteen years as a detective for the Chicago Police Department, on January 14, 2012 and at the age of 47, I still didn't know more than one member of my birth family. Or, if I did know them, I didn't know I knew them and that's another story for another time. As, far as I was concerned, my son was the only person I knew to be biologically related to me. For a variety of reasons that was sufficient until around his 20th birthday. By that time, I had solved hundreds of investigations and couldn't, didn't or certainly hadn't put the pieces together about one of the most personal cases of all; the introduction of my place into the world. Case after case in law enforcement over the course of two decades were just a handful of very important experiences that made up my journey in the span of nearly a half a century, but the impact they each would have on me was enormous.

People at some point in their life think of themselves as a detective when looking for answers. It might be the wife who thinks her husband is cheating on her, or the employee who believes someone less qualified has been promoted to a new position, or the child who knows that their sibling is the one mommy should be blaming for the mishap at home. It could be any subject matter at any age that evokes a need for an investigation. It can start at an early age for many people to look for evidence that supports their belief or denies it.

I started professionally investigating things of importance like the lives affected by a traumatic event shortly after my 23rd birthday and it took twice that age to go fact finding about what happened during the first chapter of my life. "Journey toward the light though the path may be uncertain and move forward in faith without doubt or disbelief." That was my quote and mantra as I started on the path in the year 2010 to discover more peace from the pieces. I invite you to join me in exploring my backstory and how as a detective (literally speaking), I came to the conclusion that a search and reunion with my birth family would prove to be for me the most empowering investigation of all.

1 RELINQUISHED AT BIRTH

There was much going on in 1964 all over the United States of America, but nothing more controversial than the issue of equal rights.

As far back as I can remember, I have always known that I was separated in 1964 from my biological family and adopted at the age of two. I cannot recall not knowing, or even the first time my adoptive parents told me that I was an adopted child. It's just something towards the beginning of my life that was revealed to me without any pomp and circumstance. Something else I know about 1964 is the passage of Roe vs. Wade would not occur for another nine years at the time of my birth on May 3rd.

During that time, the Beatles sang about love. Bonanza, a program about the American West was rated the best television series, and Cassius Clay became Muhammad Ali. Nelson Mandela was sentenced to life in prison on June 12th by South Africa's apartheid government just weeks before saying, "During my lifetime I have dedicated myself to this struggle of the African people...I have cherished the ideal of a democratic and free society in which all persons live together in harmony and with equal opportunities."

Not even a month later, on July 2nd, Lyndon B. Johnson signed into law landmark legislation that outlawed discrimination based on race, color, religion, sex, and natural origin. On paper, it ended across the land the unequal application of racial segregation in schools, the workplace and facilities that served the general public throughout the country as a part of the Civil Rights Movement. Dr. Martin Luther King Jr. pleaded with Johnson to further assist the movement as he prepared to lead the historic march on Selma,

Alabama in 1965. There was much going on in 1964 all over the United States of America, but nothing more controversial than the issue of equal rights.

The climate during that time consisted of the Civil Rights Movement being strongly felt throughout the country. Peace marches were being conducted in nearly every major city in the south and Dr. Martin Luther King Jr. would later lead those same demonstrations in other segregated cities in the north like Chicago, my place of birth. When President Johnson signed the new Civil Rights law, also referred to as the "Public Accommodation Act," I was just shy of two months old and in foster care by then. In the 1960's, foster care agencies didn't quickly allow for permanent placement. Adoption by foster parents was a rigorous task and often proved impossible based on strict guidelines and requirements.

Foster parents were on the frontline of this movement of adoption. They took other people's children into their homes on a temporary, permanent, formal and informal basis. According to Clare L. McClausand in *Children of Circumstance*, "In the 1960s, there were twice as many children in foster care than in the previous decade. During that time, at least two developments distanced adoption from foster care: the growth of public social welfare services and a new consciousness about the plight of African-American, mixed-race, older, Native-Americans, developmentally delayed, physically disabled, and other hard-to-place children." By definition from AdoptionHistoryProject.com, foster parents were expected to provide havens of safety and love for children at risk, but they were also responsible for keeping children in contact with relatives and agency workers. Adopters, on the other hand, were more affluent. They paid for the services they received, overwhelmingly preferred babies and young children whose racial identities matched their own, and were legally entitled to manage their families without supervision after court decrees were issued. Adoption spelled permanence, but the price of that permanence was the social obliteration of natal ties.

I trust that you are feeling the pulse of the energy in America – the "land of the free and the home of the brave" – during the time of my birth. Out of the gate, I wanted to address the issue of equal rights when writing this book, because in the 1960's only a few states in this country would deem it fit and necessary for adoptees to possess their original birth certificate (OBC). I was born in one of those states that denied the right for adoptees to access a simple piece of paper.

Whenever I consider where I am and where I'm headed, the past or backstory is always of significant purpose. It lays a foundation or root cause as to why certain events followed one after another. I typically don't stare or park in the past concerning my set of circumstances. I like to choose my gaze or give my attention to what is going on in the present moment and live in the now. I glance at the past for encouragement, inspiration and reassurance that everything is working out for me, because it truly is as it is for you too. While it's true, that when my GPS on my cellphone has to re-route me because I missed an exit or a turn, it never asks, "What happened before now? Where or why did you turn left instead of right? When did you not hear or understand me?" The system is simply designed to just give me new directions, so I can proceed to the route. My navigational system is only concerned with getting me to my programmed destination.

My arrival at a place is actually less important to me than my journey, because life itself is just that: A journey, not a destination. We spend far more time getting from point A to point B in life based on our preparation or practice of a thing than making our actual arrival. It was Ernest Hemingway who said, "It is good to have an end to journey towards; but it is the journey that matters in the end." We make plans to fall consecutively behind each other in an attempt to keep up with our desires. The time spent going and hopefully growing along the way seems to be so much bigger than whatever the thing that we're moving towards.

That is where my observation of other people's past experiences comes into play. I can reflect on the growth, wisdom and successes of others to give me added momentum for my next set of circumstances. It's funny how that is as relevant today as it was a quarter of a century ago.

In 1964, the United States counted 255,000 foster children and in Illinois, the Chicago Child Care Society (CCCS) had 370 of them. At the time, CCCS was one of the leading adoption agencies in the Chicago area and also managed foster care services to hundreds of families. They worked with Family Services Bureau of the United Charities to facilitate adoptions because unwed mothers often sought assistance from various social service networks. CCCS received a number of referrals from other agencies during that time period to help with adoption placement while simultaneously placing children into permanent homes from within their own foster care program.

"One of the most difficult programs to evaluate was the foster care program, long considered the core of the agency's (CCCS) work."[1] It was in 1964 when CCCS experienced the most adoptions. Fifty-four children were placed into homes. The referral program ended its cooperative efforts with the Family Service Bureau of United Charities (FSB) in 1964 after a twenty-year relationship. FSB reshaped its program to lend services to the younger and unmarried mother still living at home with her parents. This resulted in fewer babies being placed for adoption through CCCS. "In addition to adoptions in the 1960's, the CCCS was "critically examined for their productivity and efficiency in providing foster and day care." [2]

The CCCS was initially called the Chicago Orphan Asylum. They accepted children without regard for race, religion or nationality and assisted in finding permanent homes for many of them when only a few other such institutions existed throughout the country.

I never labeled myself as an orphan, because I was never led to believe that I was abandoned, cast away, left or deserted by my biological parents. Nor was I under the impression that they were deceased during the time of my relinquishment. However, the term orphan is sometimes used to describe a person who is separated from both parents, and in that case, I fit the bill, and I'm not the least bit offended by the term. In the award-winning movie, Cider House Rules (1999), an orphanage in St. Cloud, Maine during the early 1900's was often frequented by couples looking to adopt younger children. After watching the film, I discovered that the orphans at times shared their home with pregnant women who came there looking to have an illegal abortion by their main caretaker (a licensed physician), as depicted in the movie. The story of Homer Wells growing up as an orphan and learning the medical profession at the hands of his informally adopted father (Dr. Wilbur Larch) before moving away to discover himself is a story about the mysteries of life unfolding in the simplest and not so simplest of ways. I learned in this film about how people somehow fit into the world with each other when they least expect it. There are times in the story that you get a glimpse into the spirit of an orphan/foster child before he leaves the institution known previously as home.

The novel by John Irving, upon which the movie is based, goes deeper into the difficulty of finding homes for orphan babies in those times. Dr. Larch says, "Sometimes a woman simply can't make herself stop a pregnancy, she feels the baby is already a baby—from the first speck—and she has to have it—although she doesn't want it and she can't take care of it—and so she comes to us and has her baby here. She leaves it here, with us. She trusts us to find it a home." I found myself identifying with the children of this story and it ranks as one of my all time favorites, so on some level I do relate to being an orphan, though I never lived in an orphanage.

At the age of three months and one day old on August 4th, 1964, the bodies of Civil Rights workers Michael Schwerner, Andrew Goodman and James E. Chaney were discovered in an earthen Mississippi dam. By October 14th, Dr. King had been announced as a winner of the Nobel Peace Prize, and on November 3rd, President Johnson defeated Barry Goldwater to win the presidency. On December 22nd, Sam Cooke's, "A Change is Gonna Come" was released for his final album,"Ain't That Good News" after his death that year. Another change was coming for me, but not for another two years.

As my 1st birthday was rapidly approaching, Malcolm X was assassinated in Harlem at the Audubon Ballroom on February 21st. Dr. M.L. King Jr. led the march on Selma that culminated on March 25th, and the number of demonstrators that day swelled to

25,000 at the steps of Montgomery, Alabama's capital. By August 6th, in the presence of Dr. King and other civil rights leaders, President Johnson signed the Voting Rights Act of 1965. Recalling the outrage on Selma, President Johnson called the right to vote, "the most powerful instrument ever devised by man for breaking down injustice and destroying the terrible walls which imprison men because they are different from other men". [3]

A few days later, Dr. King, in his annual address to the SCLC (Southern Christian Leadership Council) noted that "Montgomery led to the Civil Rights Act of 1957 and 1960; Birmingham inspired the Civil Rights Act of 1964, and Selma produced the voting rights legislation of 1965." [4] All three significant events occurred in Alabama, the twenty-second state. All this was happening in the country while I remained with my foster family somewhere in Chicago throughout 1964 and 1965.

It was on January 26th, 1966, when Dr. King moved into an apartment in a Chicago slum, announcing his intention to start a campaign against discrimination there. This was in response to the increasing unrest in Northern cities over prejudice and de facto segregation. That was a few months before an average middle-aged black couple living in the Washington Heights community on the far south side of Chicago decided that they wanted to adopt a child. These two people (Halscy and Clarice Ghoston) were both employed by the Board of Education, one as a librarian's assistant and the other as a custodian. They set their sights on starting a family the non-traditional way, through adoption.

In today's language, they would be considered "prospective adoptive parents" (PAPs). They were subjected to a home study which included an inspection of your home, your background, your financial ability to raise a child, your parenting skills or tools, your marriage and many other aspects of your life. Their assignment was to prove that they were able to care for me.

On July 11, 1966 for the first time, I met two people who I would soon start calling Mom and Dad. This is from a note in a book my mother kept for me labeled "School Days RECORDS AND MEMORIES." At that time, I was called Bonnie.

8

Mon. 1:00, 7-11-66 Met Bonnie. 1st impression – Tall, sweet, a mind of her own. Friendly later on.

Fri. – 7-15-66 Saw her again – in her home, sweet – friendly

Sat. - 7-16-66 I picked her up – took her home - Halscy & I brought her back

Sun. – 7-17-(66) We picked her up – kept her all day – cried when we took her back

Mon. – 8-18-(66) Mrs. Novak (social worker) & I picked her up early – moved for good No crying – played with…talked – likes baths

2nd week Bonnie still asks occasionally about other parents

5th week A return visit – pointed to me & said, "that's mama?" – she (foster mother) answered "Yes" and sighed. "All's well." No more asking about them. No tears – Plays better by herself.

I believe it was early on and wonder if it was at the age of two years old when a companion developed on the inside of me who I knew would never relinquish me; she would never leave me in the care of someone else. That invisible entity would always be close enough to talk, listen, fuss, agree, disagree, laugh, frown, smile and comfort me. There came a time when it didn't matter as much that others would come and go or move me around. I became Bonnie's Jennifer or Jennifer's Bonnie, either way they were both a part of my being and counterparts throughout my journey.

In twelve months time, in 1967, it was official through an adoption decree that I was a Ghoston. Patrick McMahon, an adoptee and the author of *Becoming Patrick* wrote: "Of course, I've known in order to be chosen, I had to be unchosen. Surely every adopted child figures that out." Meanwhile in another home, some of my original family members were living with the truth that they had un-chosen me during my first year of life.

Adoptive parents, adoptees and birth parents make up "the adoption triad" in the adoption community. This refers to the fact that the three participants in the adoption process are connected to one another. I prefer the term "adoption circle." It better describes the overlap or continuity between members of the triad. The adoption community also embraces the term "constellation" when referring to the triad, because it means the group or cluster of related things, and in an adoption, there are many more than just three sides.

In the 1960's, according to Ronald Nydam, author of *Adoptees Come Of Age*, "The truth that could set the adoptee free, set the birth parent free and could set the adoptive parent free was held captive to concerns about shame and embarrassment...and no one was set free."

All or some members of the constellation typically feel a sense of loss at sometime in their life. The adoptee feels a loss from being relinquished by the original or birth mother. Adoptive parents feel the loss of fertility and genetic continuity. The birth mother feels the loss of their relinquished child. Separation or loss is usually followed by grief. There is not a single grief definition that covers everything, but I'll just go with, "the normal and natural emotional reaction to loss" (from TryGriefRecoveryMethod.com). Grief can be accompanied by anger, guilt, anxiety, sadness, and despair. Grieving periods can be short or long term. Just ask some birth mothers, and many will tell you that they do not believe that they made the decision to surrender or relinquish their baby. Ann Fessler, in The Girls Who Went Away, writes: "Many women, even those in their twenties, followed the only path that was available to them – the one prescribed by society, social workers, and parents."

One thing seems consistent among birth mothers decades after their life-defining experience is wanting to know the answer to three questions: Is the person I gave birth to still alive? Are they in good health? What sort of life did they have with their adoptive family?

During my third year of life, a woman who I wouldn't meet and become dear friends with for another thirty years relinquished her son to adoption. Her name is Gail and her son is Andrew. He was adopted at the age of four and answered to the name of Terry given to him at birth by Gail. Interestingly, Andrew discovered original birth records in his home at the age of ten, which identified his mother's name and he vowed to locate her in the future. During his pre-teens, he began a limited search for Gail despite feeling deeply loved by his parents and experiencing a very good childhood. His on and off again search over the next several years ended in 2003 when he was able to reunite with Gail.

Andrew had one important question for Gail, "Why?". She was able to provide him with answers. Their reunion was initially clouded by hesitation and reluctance on Andrew's part due to his thoughts of "the bottom falling out", but the bond they formed over a six-month period erased all of his fears. He met other biological family members and went on to connect with people he had never known. Andrew's other question had to do with the identity of his birth father and though he wasn't yet able to receive full closure in that area, he expressed great contentment in now knowing Gail.

There is little mention of birth fathers prior to the 1970s, because they didn't have many rights, and most did not seem too interested in being a part of the circle based on societal views of unwed pregnancy. Most birth fathers' names failed to even appear on birth certificates until after 1970 unless the biological parents were married to each other. However, there is little evidence to support birth fathers feeling any less ambivalent about the surrendering of their child.

In the film *The Forty-Year Secret* by Mary Anne Alton, one couple rekindle a high school romance and search for their daughter. This video is very informative about teenage pregnancy and the lives torn apart in the sixties. Many pregnant teens lost their babies to adoption and were told to get over it and pretend that they were never pregnant. Birth mothers surrendered their newborns and hoped for the best. Adoptive parents met the criteria set forth by private agencies or state-funded organizations and looked forward to bonding with their adopted children. But there was nothing that helped any of the members of the constellation deal with their grief.

Adoptive parents come from all walks of life and have a story to tell of their own, and no two stories are the same. My parents were unable to conceive a child and found adoption to be the solution to starting their family. They were trailblazers in a sense, because prior to 1966, neither side of my parents' family had formally adopted a child. In black culture, children are not typically adopted from an entirely different family. Someone within the family usually assumes responsibility for another family member's child when the parent(s) opt for an adoption plan. That was the case for both Yvette and Danita who remained with their birth families in the 1960s.

Yvette was adopted by extended family members within her biological family. Her formal adoption was completed while she was still in the hospital and she recalls being told about it at the age of ten. Yvette's birth mom was in her life throughout her youth and she grew up knowing her entire birth family. She describes a wonderful childhood with all family members and wouldn't change a thing about having loving parents and her birth mother in her life.

Danita went to live with her maternal grandparents as if they were her birth parents. She learned of her kinship adoption at the age of seven and subsequently went back to her birth mother and father for a period of time. She has full siblings who arrived after the initial plan made by her family when her parents were un-married teenagers. She has always been with her extended biological family members. During childhood, she had contact with her biological parents, siblings, aunts, uncles, cousins, etc. and her family arrangement was actually quite consistent with black culture.

Formal and informal kinship adoptions were common years ago for a variety of reasons and are perhaps some of the first open adoptions. While there are some challenges unique to these open adoptions such as establishing boundaries and the family gatherings, it still provides powerful advantages. "Whenever children must leave their birth parents, the trauma of separation is softened when they can remain with people, places, and cultures familiar to them."[5] -

Even back then, practices varied in different places. Some adoptive parents have biological children before and after adopting a child. And still others desire to provide a home to children from foster care, as in my case.

I believe children are resilient and tend to live in the now. Years later, when my mother shared with me a question I asked a week or so into my permanent placement from foster care, I realized how quickly I had accepted on some level that everything was working out for my good. "When am I going home (referring to my foster family)?" I asked. My mother responded, "You are home." I said, "Ok" and continued to play. It would be over a decade before I would ask more questions and seek to understand just what my closed adoption really meant in the world and to me.

Throughout the 1960s, adoptions in Illinois were closed, and the record of the biological parents is kept sealed or a secret. During the 1930s, 40s, and 50s, social workers began sealing birth and adoption records. Closed adoptions are not the same as closed records, although they are closely related issues. The rationale for the change in practice was guided by the attitudes, mores, and myths of the time. Secrecy surrounding adoptions were believed to protect the constellation. I believe that something other than the truth ultimately protects no one. Other reasons given for the closure of records, past and present, according to Researchetcinc.com include:

- protection from intrusion into the privacy of all parties;
- protection from blackmail;
- protecting the adoptee from knowledge of disturbing acts surrounding their birth – incest, rape, etc.
- enhancing the adoptee's feelings of permanency;
- enhancing the family's stability and preserving the nuclear family;
- encouraging the use of adoption instead of abortion, black market placement, child abuse, or neglect.

Many social workers and adoption experts throughout the country in the 1960s believed that some information should be given to adoptive parents about the birth family, but they didn't necessarily agree on how much should be disseminated by agencies. This seems to support the belief that adoptive parents had an upper hand or at least were the individuals within the constellation who maintained the most power and protection. Non-identifying information such as nationality, physical characteristics, education, occupation, health factors, abilities and talents were all considered important facts to share with adopting parents. The issue was whether to reveal information that would be viewed as negative, such as criminal behavior, alcoholism, mental illness, and/or illegitimacy (the status of a child born to parents who are not legally married to each other). During this time, the Child Welfare League of America still did not consider it "necessary and desirable" to give a physical description of the birth parents."[6]

All of this secrecy by way of sealed records of what information to share and what to withhold began to spark much debate. It would not be until around my 7th birthday when a social worker, Annette Baran, M.S.W., who had initially embraced closed records, would begin to turn the tide on closed adoptions. Baran, a psychotherapist and co-author of *The Adoption Triangle* and Betty Jean Lifton (writer, adoptee, adoption reform advocate, and author of *Twice Born: memoirs of an adopted daughter*) were two extraordinary women in the adoption community. They worked fearlessly for years to create open adoption and unsealed records. Baran once said, "Why does everything have to be a secret? What is all that nonsense about?" She went on to say that "If we have open adoptive placement, we wouldn't have sealed records. We wouldn't need to seal the records. They go hand in hand. It's time to let the records become unsealed."

While only time would later allow for the pioneers of adoption reform to start a movement and change the system, my mother was told by the social worker to tell me of my adoption according to the degree I could understand it. She insisted that my mother diminish the shame associated with adoption by not keeping it a secret. My mother would say things like, "You're in your new home and you have a new family now. I'm your new mama." She continued this practice throughout my childhood as advised by the social worker, but that does not imply that she was comfortable with any questions I may have had about my birth family. My social worker also urged the Ghostons to continue calling me "Bonnie." It was my name given at birth and the one I had been answering to while in foster care for two years. My parents did as advised, but quickly introduced my new name, Jennifer. I would learn over time to consider my birth name as a nickname. I know people who didn't realize until entering elementary school that their nickname wasn't their birth name. I felt I had something in common with others never separated from their birth families.

When some people think about adoption, they envision a closed adoption in which the identities of the adoptive family and birth mother remain confidential, with no contact prior to or after the placement of the child. For many generations, it was a common practice to keep adoptions closed and deny adoptees access to their original birth certificate (OBC) or any information relative to their birth family throughout their lives. My OBC was a part of a file somewhere, but under no circumstances by law was it to be made available to me at any time.

In my home growing up, there was no file of non-identifying information or otherwise relative to my foster care or adoption being retained by my parents, or if there was, I was never privy to it. If there had been a file, it would have likely contained two birth certificates, because that's the case for formal adoptions. The OBC contains the names of the birth parent(s) and delivered baby. This record in Illinois and in most other states was sealed to prevent an adoptee from knowing their true identity and original family. The OBC is considered to be an unofficial document and can never take the place of the amended birth certificate (ABC). I find it interesting that in Alaska and Kansas, adopted persons have always had access to their OBCs upon reaching the age of majority. What makes the adoptees in these states any different from those of us born elsewhere?

The OBC in most states is retained and accessed only by a court order. That is a direction issued by a court or a judge requiring a person to do or not do something. The legal proceeding of adoption is so complete that the issued ABC for the adoptee shows the adoptive parents' names as the child's mother and father at the time of birth. The ABC belonging to an adoptee contains his/her new name and the names of the adoptive parents. My birth date and other information contained on the original certificate was believed to be truthfully carried over to my new official document, stating Jennifer Dyan Ghoston as my new name. The name Bonnie doesn't appear anywhere on this new birth certificate. My ABC was an official document, created just after my 3rd birthday, and my OBC would never again be useful in the eyes of government who had once been quoted as saying, "Tell the whole truth and nothing but the truth so help you God".

It's interesting to note while we're on the issue of OBCs that on April 26, 2011, the White House released President Barack Obama's long form birth certificate for the world to see upon the request of people who questioned his citizenship. We have Donald Trump to thank for this disclosure by having repeatedly said that President Obama should show his OBC as proof that he was born in the United States.

President Obama is not an adoptee and the state of his birth (Hawaii) has open birth records. But, it was at this time that members of the adoption constellation began to speculate about the outcome of the request if President Obama had been an adoptee and had only been able to produce an Amended Birth Certificate (ABC). On Facebook, dated May 12, 2011, Mara Parker, Trinidad, California responded to a *Wall Street Journal* publication dated April 28, 2011 about the incident. She wrote:

"I am glad that President Obama was able to obtain a copy of his original long-form birth certificate to prove that he was born in the U.S. However, if President Obama had been born and adopted in almost any of the states in the U.S., he still would not be able to produce his original birth certificate for the public or even for his own viewing. By law, he would only be able to produce an amended birth certificate (ABC). An amended birth certificate is issued at the finalization of a person's adoption. This birth certificate replaces a person's birth name with a new name and the natural parents' names,

with those of the adoptive parents. Once an ABC is issued, a person is kept from viewing or possessing a truthful documentation of birth. The original birth certificate is sealed forever. I wish President Obama had been adopted so that the country could see how discriminatory it is to seal an adopted person's birth certificate and replace it with a falsified one."

I've given you some foundation about a set of ideas and systems in place during the 1960s. There are some other beliefs to explore that were held during such a powerful decade. Before you go a bit deeper with me beyond the subject of separation, loss and grief through relinquishment, I strongly urge you to get a feel for the history during the time of your entry into the world. Take a moment to reflect on what was going on locally, nationally and internationally when you arrived on this earth. Your experience may be similar to mine or altogether different. Whatever the case, I believe that it will give you added insight to what energy drew you here and perhaps your purpose for however long you grace this planet. This is an exercise in seeing how your perspective about people, places and things is jointly based on the attitudes of those around you. We are all connected to the important decisions that were made some time ago, and needless to say, they affect our lives today. However, it's all about perspective and perception. What is yours, and is it serving you or not? Give it some thought and keep in mind that a momentum is going to build in the chapters that follow as it relates to my journey and yours. I thank you in advance for staying the course with me as we move away from anything shallow about a deeper conversation.

[1] Children of Circumstance, Clare L. McClausand, p. 195

[2] Children of Circumstance, McClausand, p. 194

[3] Kingencyclopedia.stanford.edu

[4] Kingencyclopedia.stanford.edu

[5] Telling the Truth to Your Adopted or Foster Child/Making Sense of the Past by Keefer & Schooler, 2000

[6] The Adoption Triangle, Sorosky, Baran, Pannor p. 36

2 ALLOWING ADOPTION TO MAKE SENSE

I would not fully understand the gravity of being apart from my original family for many years to come.

Once all settled into my new and final home during the summer of my 3rd year on earth in the year 1967, I was labeled an only child. I now lived in an affluent neighborhood where whites raced to move out as blacks increasingly moved into the area. "For Sale" signs went up on lawns all over the city in previously predominately white areas as black families signed the documents to close on their houses and become new homeowners. Chicago was already known for being one of the most segregated cities in the north, but seeing is believing according to my mother. My parents were excited to own their first house, but most white people simply did not want to live around blacks for whatever reason and they were fleeing to other places. Stereotypes and racism are to blame for the majority of fears people experience about other ethnic groups. When I tell you that the families on my block kept their lawns manicured, believed in law and order, wanted the best education for their children, went to church, paid their taxes, worked legitimate jobs every day, and wanted the same things that white people wanted for their families, I mean it.

There were only two white families who remained on the block when I was a child, and they lived across the street from us. I believe that they really didn't see black people moving in the neighborhood as a reason to pack up and move away. On the same side of the street just a couple of doors south was another black family who had moved there about two years before my parents.

They were among the other black families who also wanted a better quality of life in Chicago and chose a section of Washington Heights. Their youngest daughter, Paulette, seemed to look out for me. When I was teased or my jump rope taken by a bully, Paulette would take up for me just like a big sister. She called me Bonnie until such time that my mother insisted that she start calling me Jennifer. This particular family provided a helping hand to my parents. In my mind's eye, I can still see Paulette's parents waving, saying hello, sharing a smile and being genuinely kind to my new family.

One month before my 4th birthday, Dr. Martin Luther King Jr. was assassinated on April 4th at the Lorraine Motel in Memphis, Tennessee. He was fatally shot while standing on the balcony outside of his room. I can only imagine the emotional climate felt all over the world when this information was covered by the evening news. I had officially been a Ghoston for nearly a year and was preparing to attend the Auburn Park preschool about two miles from my home. It had been suggested that I was ready to start school early, but my mother insisted on waiting until the September after my fifth birthday. From all accounts, I had a smooth development at Auburn Park, but I really loved the following year in kindergarten with Mrs. Webster for half a day Monday through Friday. I have memories of attending elementary school just around the corner from my house as a five year old. One of my earliest recollections of testing the system and being rebellious during that time involved having to receive the dreaded school shots administered with a huge gun-like needle to the top of my left arm. A lasting mark has stood the test of time.

There were two kindergarten classes: A.M. and P.M. For a time, I attended school in the P.M. On one occasion, I received a pinned-on note from Mrs. Webster stating that kindergartners were to be present in the A.M. on a future date for mandatory vaccinations. According to my mother's records, I stood 46 ½ inches tall and weighed forty-six pounds. Some time between getting the note attached to my clothing and arriving home for my mother to receive it, I threw it away. The day came and went for vaccinations and my parents were soon notified that I hadn't received my shots. The truth about the note being discarded by me would be the first of much lying and deceit to my parents over the years in an effort to avoid consequences, or so I thought. This was the first of many lessons that reminds me that we are "free to choose, but not free from the consequences of our choices." And yes, I did eventually receive all of my vaccinations as required by law back then while never liking Mrs. Webster any less.

As a child, it seemed like people were reluctant to discuss my adoption, and when it did come up in conversation, they seemed to tip toe around it. "So, you know that you were adopted? How does it feel?" they would ask. "I feel fine. How should I feel?" I would inquire. "Well, do you ever wonder about finding your real parents? Do you think about what happened to your real parents? Are you sad about your real parents giving you away?" All of these questions had me wondering if I should be feeling badly or sadly about my adoption. After all, I was with my real parents, wasn't I? They were the ones loving me, caring for my needs and preparing me for life's challenges. I rather enjoyed the questions and probing, because it showed people's interest. And if they pitied me, they were at least interested in knowing more to my story. I wasn't aware of the Adopted Child Syndrome term first studied by Jean Paton in 1953, but perhaps others had given it some thought. Maybe more than a few people thought adopted children had problems in bonding, attachment disorders, lying, stealing, defiance of authority, and being prone to violence. I was only aware of the shamefulness of anyone being born out of wedlock, because that was a part of society's value system at the time.

Perhaps the greatest implication of shame being a part of the equation in adoption for me was the issue of being born illegitimate and an unwanted child. The fact that my birth family didn't keep me or gave me away was a painful thought, so I chose to view my adoption as my birth family wanting more for me than they felt they were able to provide at the time. Even as a child, I knew I had a choice in how I could view a subject, but I didn't realize just how influential I would allow others to be about me being an adoptee. I was beginning to process this subject of shame about adoption as I observed the people around me attempt to make sense of it. Black families often struggle with decisions made to separate from each other, and perhaps this is a cultural habit that relates to the days of slavery.

Part of the issue with the perception of a situation is the language used to describe a person, place or thing. Consider how changes in the language can alter perceptions within the adoption community and others. For example, an adopted child or adopted person is more often referred to as an adoptee. Some other references of those in the constellation include birth, biological, original, or first parent(s) instead of natural parents. By the age of ten, I was rather comfortable in my skin as an adoptee and grew closer with my invisible companion. I could be heard engaging in conversations with myself as long as I thought I was alone. I would ask a question out loud and answer it aloud with such ease. If I thought someone might hear me, then I would cease my chatter. I had heard that talking to oneself was fine, but answering was a different story. I did both. I rather enjoyed the verbal exchanges, and I often laughed. My companion had now been with me a long time and there was nothing to suggest that she was going to leave me. That was a good thing, because I felt wanted by my own company that would never reject or relinquish me.

"Yes, I'm adopted." I would divulge this information when asked, and on occasion volunteer it. I wasn't using the term adoptee, because I hadn't a clue about an adoption community and the terminology or jargon at that time. If there was such a group of adoptees meeting somewhere in Chicago, I knew nothing about it. If there was counseling available for members of the constellation, it wasn't discussed with me. I don't recall any conversations with my parents about it, or questions like, "How does being adopted make you feel?" I'm not saying that it didn't occur, but I was never exposed to a group setting specifically designed to develop fellowship with others who shared my experience. At the time, I was a drifter when it came to the subject of my adoption. I lacked definiteness of purpose about my identity as an adoptee.

Typically, we are allowed or able to be with others who we share something in common like members of our same sex, others of our nationality, those who share our same interests, people who you identify with because you're a part of that group. I don't ever remember being with other adoptees for the sole purpose of being with them because they were like me.

By 1976, in the 6thgrade, I was a twelve-year-old tomboy and had never played with Barbie dolls. I don't even remember painting my nails. I loved softball, riding my bike and becoming proficient at profanity like my dad. He was good at it. I wanted to drive a bus or be a taxi cab driver, because I loved being outdoors and behind a steering wheel. My dad taught me how to drive before my thirteenth birthday and I was the one who cut our grass every week. I preferred baiting hooks with night crawlers when fishing with my father, over window shopping and spending all day in department stores with my mother. I was a daddy's girl who didn't mind traveling back and forth by car to his hometown of Panola, Alabama.

When I first asked, "Where is the bathroom?" while down South in Alabama, my dad pointed at the outhouse standing alone in a field. I recall the flies and the horrible smell. The conditions in this small town of Panola, where most people were without indoor plumbing, was a world apart from the big city I knew as home in Chicago. I never complained too much about my dad's place of birth not far from the Mississippi border, because he was proud of where he and five siblings had lived until they migrated to the North for a better way of life. My dad wasn't an intellectual or artistic person. He left that in the hands of his wife, my mother.

Through my mother's attention to education, I became a strong reader and a lover of the arts. I enjoyed all kinds of music, poetry and short stories. I regularly listened to her albums by Nat King Cole, Tony Bennett, Dinah Washington, Nancy Wilson, Johnny Mathis, Billie Holiday, and especially Sam Cooke. "Live at the Copacabana on July 7th & 8th of 1964" was my favorite, because Cooke's voice was soothing on a medley when he sang, "No I'll never, never, never... treat you wrong..." Cooke's laughter made me smile. My mother and I would listen to music in the living room for hours and sometimes get up and dance.

My mother would bring discarded books home that said "Property of Wendell Phillips High School" for me to read when we couldn't get to the public library. She even enrolled me in the Evelyn

Woods Speed Reading Program. It helped me learn to read twice as many books in half the amount of time. By now, I had on countless occasions asked my parents how they felt about my adoption. I often wondered what my parents really thought about it. They were consistent each time I asked them, saying, "We couldn't have children of our own. We wanted a child and you were chosen from all the other children." I always thought, "Ok, being chosen will work for now."

In the 7th grade, I was smoking cigarettes whenever I could steal one from my dad or bum one from older friends. I was still listening to all kinds of great music. I played favorites by artists like Stevie Wonder, Elton John, Diana Ross, Bob Dylan, James Brown, Jim Croce, James Taylor, Aretha Franklin and many, many others. My dad said there were only two real singers in the world: "The Queen of Soul" and Mahalia Jackson. I always asked him to add Gladys Knight to the list, but he refused my request. It was around the turn from one decade to another that my dad was interested in obtaining his original birth certificate, so we packed our bags and headed to the capital of Alabama. He drove the entire 700-plus miles headed south down Interstate 65 towards Indianapolis, followed by Louisville, then into Nashville, and right through Huntsville, to Montgomery. When all was said and done on that journey, the state of Alabama had to create a birth certificate for my father based on the information he was able to supply them. At least he finally had a copy of his original birth certificate.

I'd like to think I was the typical pre-teen with a bit of an edge, though not really knowing where it came from. I would light up a Camel filter or a Marlboro in the neighborhood park near my home when I was supposed to be playing sports. I would join at least one other twelve-year-old friend there. She was like most of my friends who resembled more than one other relative. I thought it was so cool and perhaps envied the fact that she, her brother and sister, all looked just like their parents. I wanted to experience looking like someone in my family. I wanted to say, "I look just like so and so" even if it were a grandmother or an aunt and not my parents or a sibling. Interestingly enough, I did look like one of my first cousins on my dad's side, but it wasn't the same, because I knew I had been adopted.

People who didn't know or who forgot I was adopted were always commenting: "I knew you and your cousin were related, because you look alike." It was nice, but not the same as looking like someone related by blood. The issue of genetics seemed important as I entered 8th grade and prepared to go on to high school even though I knew several biologically related families where members didn't really look like each other. I was beginning to observe the nuances of remaining with one's biological family, but I would not fully understand the gravity of being apart from my original family for many years to come.

I didn't consciously think about being an adoptee day in and day out, but rather would be reminded of it from time to time. Occasionally someone might say, "You're adopted? Oh. Okay" and then we'd go back to talking about something else. The whole adoption issue and reuniting with my birth family didn't seem important by the time I was ready to leave high school. I was a Ghoston through and through and rarely heard the name "Bonnie" mentioned by family or friends, but that part of me was still there. When it was sparingly spoken, it sounded like someone I knew of, but didn't entirely remember. She had been silenced in a way and replaced with the routines of life. I no longer felt like I needed a constant companion as in my earlier years.

The type of shame, secrecy and lies of the 1960s were a thing of the past in many ways by the 1980s. Nearly everything related to adoption was changing slowly but surely for the better. The Roe vs. Wade decision had been in existence for a decade by 1983. Fewer and fewer babies were available for adoption in the U.S., because the stigma associated with teen pregnancy had significantly diminished from past decades. I knew of several friends in high school who became pregnant as seniors, juniors and even sophomores. They each kept their baby. In fact, these young mothers finished high school and many went on to college while raising their child. One of my friends told me, "I didn't expect to become pregnant, but my baby is the best thing that has happened to me and my family." What a difference a couple of decades made in the lives of so many families including those affected by adoption.

The Cannes Film Festival award-winning movie by Mike Leigh *Secrets and Lies* (1996) is about the closed adoption of a young black woman (Hortence) seeking her birth mother. She discovers her mother is white and the resulting chaos leads to a series of revelations. This story is breathtaking, wildly humorous, poignant, and especially heartwarming as it weaves its way through the issue of closed adoptions, shame and secrecy. I can relate to this film, especially in a scene where Hortence tells a girlfriend, "We (adoptees) choose our parents, so we can get it right."

What if we are always co-creating our circumstances and situations? Imagine having a strong desire, but not necessarily being specific about it or knowing exactly how to manifest it. Then, you decide based on what happens in your life to intentionally re-create something that's closer to what feels more comfortable for your purpose in life at this time. For a moment ignore your verbal responses and consider your vibration to every single thing going on around you. It reminds me of the research that has demonstrated how non-verbal communication is 93% more reliable than verbal communication. Body language and our energy is the best source of valid information. How would this information impact my thoughts as an adoptee in search of her birth family? For now, rest in an interlude about one of the most important parts of our identity: a given name.

Interlude: What's In a Name?

A good name is more desirable than great riches;
to be esteemed is better than silver or gold.
Proverbs 22:1

One of the first things people ask when they meet someone is "What's your name?" And when we forget a new name within a few minutes, we hope it gets repeated or we can remember it. We may even ask, "What's your name again?" It's important.

A name is a powerful part of a person's being and identity. It can be closely linked to how good we feel about ourselves. A 2010 CNN report stated, The 1960s, is responsible for expanding the pool of names. More Americans began to reject conformity and embrace individualism. "Nobody wants their kids to fit in anymore", Laura Wattenberg, founder of the book and blog, BabyNameWizard.com said. They want them to stand out. In 1960, Mary was the most popular girl name, and David the number one boy name. Jennifer made the list at #61, and Bonnie was #71. By 1970, Jennifer was #1, and Bonnie didn't make the top 100.[7]

Some people might argue that adoptive parents should refrain from changing an adoptee's name when he or she has been answering to something different for some time. My immediate family, neighbors and some friends consistently called me Bonnie until around the time I entered school. One of my cousins once said, "I didn't know why we had to stop calling you Bonnie. I like that name." She was referring to me increasingly answering to Jennifer over Bonnie at my mother's request for me to learn my new name. A friend offered this reflection: "We called you Bonnie, and then it seemed like the next day we had to start calling you Jennifer. As a child, I didn't understand why your mother would correct us if we called you Bonnie."

It means a lot that I was named at birth, because it symbolizes to me that my first mother was given an opportunity to express a part of herself to me through time, space and distance. Also, a name being given to me by the Ghostons was their gift, and I received that too. I found it interesting that several Ghoston family members spell their name with an "L," as in "Gholston." My dad always told me that it wasn't correct. Some Ghostons within the immediate family choose to spell it that way. I've deferred to my dad's belief and never thought to change it.

I have always felt a connection to my birth family through the name Bonnie. In that way, I have been able to stay connected to a piece of my beginnings. However, the two different names seem like two separate people integrated together over time. Again, I'm referring to Jennifer's Bonnie.

On a Facebook posting on the Reunion Registry page "It will happen when it's time." The importance of a name for an adoptee under a closed system resonated with me all too well, since only time would tell just how difficult, if not impossible, it is to locate someone whose name is unknown to you.

This is a post from that page that demonstrates the power of names. Christopher is an adoptee whose birth name wasn't changed upon his adoption.

"Text: My name is Christopher. I am looking for parents or siblings. I was born June 19th, 1965 in Hollywood, Florida. I was adopted at 3 years old through the Angel Guardian Home in NY.

The posting listed his full name. At last, I had a name! So, I thought about it, and decided to look on Facebook. If someone wanted to be found, I hoped that's where I would find him. There were two people with his name. The first one

obviously didn't fit. I held my breath and pulled up the second one and immediately started to sob. His profile picture was like looking at my two maternal uncles. I had found my brother! I knew it the minute I saw his picture.

Finally, I got this message on Facebook from him shortly after 5 p.m. We talked that night for almost four hours on the phone until he had to go to bed to get up for his early morning job. He was still named Christopher because he had not been adopted until he was three and lived in an orphanage In New York until then. I guess they thought it would be confusing to change his name."

After 1966, I would never again exclusively answer to the name "Bonnie." My mother was interested in changing it to either "Odessa" or "Jennifer" upon my adoption. In the end, I was named after Dyan Cannon and Cary Grant's daughter, Jennifer. If you know anything about Jennifer Grant's life, it's no wonder that my mother must have wanted an extraordinary life for me. "Her childhood was far from pedestrian. Frank Sinatra and Quincy Jones dropped by. There were riding lessons and a beloved nanny, as well as trips to Palm Springs, the Hamptons and the prince's palace in Monaco, where Jennifer played Operation with Princess Stephanie[8]."

My mother would also share with me that my middle name, Dyan, was after Dyan Cannon, because she had a certain affinity for the young actress' style. Well, I'm as far from a Cary Grant, Dyan Cannon and Jennifer Grant as you can get, but I have always liked my name.

According to Kalabarian Philosphy.com, "the name Jennifer creates a dual nature in that you can be very generous and understanding, but you can also be so candid in your expression that you create misunderstanding. You struggle with the requirement to soften your expression with tact and diplomacy and to consider the feelings of others. You have a tendency, at times, to have too many ideas on the go, and thus your efforts are scattered and many things do not reach completion. You are inclined to do in excess the things you like to do."

Kalabarian Philosphy's brief analysis of Bonnie is as follows: "Your name of Bonnie creates an intense desire for association with people and new experiences, many of which have been rather bitter. You desire change and travel and would enjoy opportunities that allowed you to be creative and to act independently, rather than to conform to system and routine. However, this name does not allow you to complete your undertakings, as farther fields always look greener. While the name Bonnie creates the urge to create harmony with people, we call attention to the fact that it causes a restless intensity that defies relaxation."

The simpler and more common definition of the name Bonnie means attractive; beautiful; sweet spirit. Jennifer is white one; fair one. Odessa means wrathful; angry man. What does your name mean and what sort of feeling does it illicit from you? I considered what my two names meant to me and felt emotionally different when I thought of one over the other: "Jennifer" (serious, smart and urban) versus "Bonnie" (fun, easy-going and Southern or country). Each name signaled something very different in my spirit, and I embraced all of it.

[7] Babycenter.com

[8] New York Times.com, June 11, 2011

3 CAGED CURIOSITY

I believe the bonds of love are formed in so many ways and are as solid as the lives that created them.

Consider the poem I discovered to best depict two sides of an adoptee being born and co-creating life through one woman and given the tools to live that life from another one.

The Legacy of an Adopted Child

Once there were two women

Who never knew each other

One you do not remember

The other you call mother

Two different lives

Shaped to make yours one

One became your guiding star

The other became your sun.

The first gave you life

And the second taught you to live in it

The first gave you a need for love

And the second was there to give it.

The other prayed for a child.

And God led her straight to you.

And now you ask me through your tears,

The age-old question

Through the years; Heredity or environment-

Which are you the product of?

Neither my darling-neither

Just two different kinds of love.

-Author unknown

I understood that I had two mothers (and maybe three if you count my foster home). Also, I knew during my teenage years that it would be a matter of time before I knew the identity of my birth family despite my mother's unfavorable thoughts about a search for them. Like the lion before meeting Dorothy in the Wizard of Oz, I lacked courage to say, "Mom, I'm going to do it. I'M GOING TO FIND MY BIRTH FAMILY." After all, it was a reasonable desire of mine. I seldom doubted that one day their identity would be known to me. The branches to my family tree were still incomplete as I approached my twenties, so I caged my curiosity.

Making a family tree in school was once a popular activity among students. It was designed to show others a chart establishing the genealogical relationships and lines of descent. It's a written record of ancestry, but it's not so simple for an adoptee under a closed system. During my childhood, I had no reason or ability to list anyone on both sides of a family tree other than the descendants of my parents, Clarice Lee Ghoston and Halscy Ghoston. A tree has roots, and that's where I would eventually list my biological family once I knew of them. The part of the tree visible was my mother's mother and father: Anna Mae Dampier and George Lee would be placed on branches like people with their original family. My father's mother and father, Rhoda Gholston Saxon and Colin Gholston, would be placed on the other side of the tree above ground. I imagined the name of my birth mother and her parents going underground as the roots of my tree. I hoped one day to learn of my birth father's side of the tree to be placed underground too. An extended and completed family tree for me was pending during the 1980s and my connection to my Ghoston family was sufficient and enough, because I had no more information about the other part or side of myself.

When my father's mother passed in 1982, I learned more about his side of the family. I remember her being unlike what I would hope for from a grandmother. She was reserved, quiet and appeared disinterested in children. I imagined a grandmother baking cookies, having play dates, much laughter, repeated hugs, kisses and plenty of I love yous. Those things were less than a decade away towards my child from his grandmother. My relationship with my father's mother would be the first of many examples of why you don't take things personally. It is seldom if ever about me when people act like they do. It's about them. I can totally relate to a Daniell Koepke quote "The truth is that the way other people treat us isn't about us—it's about them and their own struggles, insecurities, and limitations. You don't have to allow their judgment to become your truth. You may not be able to control what other people say or how they act, but you can always choose how you treat yourself."

There were so many relatives made known to me on the day of my father's mother's funeral. Cousins and other kin seemed to accept me without any outward issue of my being an adoptee. I wondered if family members in secret discussed my adoption. They most likely had private conversations about my birth family relinquishing me to an unknown family. I can only imagine what my Ghoston family thought about my original family, but I believed that everyone loved me. It didn't matter to me what they thought about them. Whether they disliked, resented or misunderstood my birth family's decision to place me with another family made no never-mind to me. It was never openly discussed and I'm glad about that. Some things are better left unspoken.

I physically looked like my parents could have conceived me. My mother had a dark complexion with keen features and my father was light-skinned with fuller features, so there wasn't anything out of the ordinary with my medium complexion and facial features. Some people had light complexions when their siblings were dark skinned and vice versa. There were times that I could not readily identify biological connections among people of the same bloodline. Some people start to look like one another just because they spend so much time together. Similar mannerisms and body language between family members can form over time. It was easy for me to ignore that I had another family somewhere in the world that I looked like because I naturally fit into the Ghoston family.

I was often told "You look like, a Ghoston. I see it in the eyes." People would forget that I was adopted, but adoptees do not forget it. It's a life-long part of our identity. It is a life-long process. The missing pieces and lack of biological continuity are obvious beyond being asked at the doctor's office about your medical history. It's the way I can readily observe other families never separated from their original members – especially siblings who have been together throughout their lives. There is a connection that is evident in the family energy. Even in reunion, people can't make up past years and hundreds of experiences due to their separation from the family to create a physical bond that takes time. It was tempting to take the perspective that "relinquishment, separation and adoption shouldn't have happened to me. The truth is "Why not me?" I am not a victim, nor do I claim victimhood of any sort. I was simply the result of heredity and environment from two different families.

Nurture and nature are sometimes pitted against one another. I believe that nurture isn't opposite nature. They can go hand in hand, and I'm proof of that. At birth, we bring physical qualities over from a countless number of ancestors and from there the environment influences our personalities. I had no reference point yet concerning my characteristics by nature or heredity passed down from one generation to the next, so I was curious. I wanted to know more about my nature. I consider it valuable information. People who are not adoptees are able to identify some of the reasons why they are the way they are, because of inherited physical traits. The one thing I know for certain is my nature was positively influenced by my nurture and that is what's most important.

Love is always the winner in the end. In time, I realized that, as Troy Dunn, from the television show, The Locator wrote, "The people who love you when you need it are your family". I believe the bonds of love are formed in so many ways and are as solid as the lives that created them.

"Humans look at their children in a screwy way. Most humans feel possessive of their children. When they were never meant to possess them. They were just providing an avenue through which they could come forth. The family that surrounds you is your vibrational family, and sometimes it is your blood family, but often it is not. So, it makes no difference whatsoever how you come together; law of attraction brings it about. We would work everyday to blur the lines of family in terms of ownership or belonging. The only thing that is relevant is now you're here. Your relationship with who you really are, that's all that's relevant."

I hadn't yet heard this quote from an Abraham-Hicks book in the 1980s, but it can best describe how I was beginning to process my adoption experience before my 19th birthday. I wasn't the least bit angry or resentful about being relinquished by my birth family. I was certain that they had a reasonable explanation, whether I agreed with it or not. My attention was primarily focused on my having a right and a privilege to be here, as the *Desiderata* poem from 1692 found in Old Saint Paul's Church of Baltimore explains. These excerpts spoke to me:

Speak your truth quietly and clearly

And listen to others...

Be Yourself...

Be gentle with yourself.

You have a right to be here

And whether or not it is clear to you,

No doubt the universe is unfolding as it should.

Therefore be at peace with God.

Whatever you conceive Him to be,

And whatever your labors an aspirations,

In the noisy confusion of life

Keep at peace with your soul.

With all its sham, drudgery and broken dreams,

It is still a beautiful world...

My status as an adoptee in a loving family and being a vibrational match was a separate issue from being denied the right to know the identity of my birth family. My only concern was having the right to information about my history, my birth story and a reunion. It was clear to me that I wasn't to be possessed like property by anyone, as the closed adoption system suggested, by perpetuating secrets about my first family connection. I had an equal right to my original birth certificate and to know my origins, since it was my desire, just like other people who were never separated from their birth families.

I entered my freshman year of college in the same year my paternal grandmother and maternal grandfather made their transition and got right into gear as a psychology major. Michael Jackson's Thriller became one of the best-selling albums of all time. The second single released from that album, and my all time favorite, "Billie Jean" would move me to dance each time I played it. As I enjoyed all the tracks from Michael's sixth solo album, I was focused on getting Harold Washington elected as Chicago's first black mayor and keeping up with all my courses. That year, Chicago saw the largest black turnout to vote ever recorded in the city's history. Washington was elected to the mayoral office and I was elated about it. I was having a love affair with every single one of my Black Studies classes. I learned that you don't have to hate other races to love your own more. I discovered Black Nationalism for the first time and how to write short stories. I loved poetry, and Professor Sterling D. Plumpp saw my potential. He encouraged me to realize my true passion as a writer by the time I completed my first year of college. I started writing poetry and later had a poem published in Shoptalk, a cosmetology magazine.

By 1983, music was my thing and hits were being released one after another to keep me grooving to the sound of my own drum. Everything was upbeat, and music, along with comedy, seemed to be the two things in my toolbox that made me feel good. I loved George Clinton's *"Atomic Dog,"* *"Little Red Corvette"* by Prince, *"Ain't Nobody"* by Rufus Featuring Chaka Khan, and *"Sweet Dreams"* by the Eurythmics. The lyrics of that song ("Hold your head up. Keep your head up...moving on") said it best. It was my favorite song and I bumped it loud on my boom box along the beautiful lakefront of Chicago throughout that summer. In my solitude, if I wasn't listening to music, I was laughing it up with Richard Pryor and Redd Foxx albums. The sometimes over-the-top material and comedic timing by those two was the best.

Throughout the 1980s, I embraced the outdoors of Chicago during June, July and August. December, January, February and March were a different story. The brutal single-digit temperatures, a foot of snow and icy roads made Californians wonder why anyone would choose to live there. It has snowed enough times in Chicago during my birthday month of May for me to wonder the same thing too. A friend in Los Angeles once sent me a picture of herself sitting on the hood of an automobile dressed in summer clothing on Christmas day. For a long time, I couldn't understand why she didn't have a need for a coat, hat, scarf and gloves during the winter like me. She, on the other hand had never seen snow in person.

Chicago is truly a great city to visit, but has always been known as a gangster town. As far back as the Al Capone days during the 1920s, it has for sometime been a place where violence was no stranger. Yet, with all of its history of crime bosses, street gangs, political corruption and segregation, I was glad to be born there. At least, I believed I was born there as noted on my amended birth certificate. As a young adult, I had no intention of leaving anytime soon. I was a Chicagoan to the bone and accepted that I could finish my education, begin my career, start my own family and make a decent niche in my hometown.

What made it even better in the summer before my 19th birthday was my enjoyment of a close relationship with a former high school classmate who would in five years become my lawful wedded husband. He was born a day before me. Andre had never been separated from his original family, and his mother was one of the unwed teenagers of the 1960s who kept him upon his birth. I often thought she probably had never considered relinquishing him. She had likely always known with the help of her family that she would find a way to take care of her first born. His family was from Kosciusko, MS. and it would take me years to correctly pronounce the small town where Oprah Winfrey was also born.

Life was good, meaningful, and above all quite interesting as I began to take notice of how pieces to life's puzzle come together to form the big picture. That same year, Michael Jordan signed with the Chicago Bulls and was rapidly becoming a household name. I even got to meet him and take a photo at an NYE party after his decision to play for the NBA. That was when you could still get close enough to touch him. Meanwhile, I was still a student at UIC, and there were plenty of others besides Professor Plumpp who were motivating me to continue my education while working a part time job.

I worked for the hair care manufacturer Soft Sheen Products in the finance department to support myself. I had been there over three years when one morning, after getting off a bus at my stop in front of the company, things took a turn. I was motioned by the bus driver that he would wait for me to cross the street in front of him. The next thing I knew, I was thrown up in the air and landed on the hood of a woman's car. I slid off and hit the pavement headfirst. I rushed to get up so, I wouldn't get hit again. A few Soft Sheen employees came over to me and insisted that I remain still. I saw and felt the blood gushing from my head and received medical attention from my co-workers until the ambulance arrived on the scene.

My mother and her tears made me realize the seriousness of my condition. She rode with me to the hospital, because that's what mothers do. They wipe your bumps, scrapes, bruises, dry your eyes, and give you comfort in hundreds of different ways for a thousand different times. They nurse you back to health. Mothers make sure you are fine and tell you "Everything is going to be okay." My mother would do this over and over again throughout my life. It reminded me of Bob Marley's song, *"Three Little Birds"*: "Don't worry about a thing, cause every little thing is gonna be alright." I sang that verse and the chorus often: "Rise up this morning, smile with the rising sun. Three little birds pitched by my doorstep singing sweet songs of melodies pure and true saying this is my message to you. Don't worry bout a thing, cause every little thing gonna be alright. I won't worry."

I needed thirteen stiches to my forehead before my mother insisted that I be transferred to a better hospital. The closest emergency room to my accident wasn't good enough for her only daughter. I had a dislocated right shoulder and a fractured clavicle. By day two of healing, my face was black and blue. My mother and father were there to make sure I got the proper medical attention. I looked like I had been hit hard by a car, but received excellent care as I recuperated from my injuries. My mother had once again shown me during this hurdle in life that she loved and cared for me, so how in the world could I respond when she would say, "Why would you want to search for your birth mother? I'm your mom. We're your family." I always told her, "Okay, I understand."

She felt threatened by the idea of being replaced by another mother; someone who hadn't been there through my ups and downs. I couldn't articulate the importance of my desire to know my total self no more than by saying, Maybe she's right. It's not the time. It's not that important. Besides, I need more evidence to support the significance and importance of finding my birth family.

In reality, what more did I need than the right to know and make the connections with my start in life? What my mother didn't understand is that my desire to find my birth family had nothing to do with her or my Ghoston family. It had everything to do with me, and my first family.

How could my mother understand my desire to reconnect with my first family? She had never been separated from hers. She couldn't possibly know what it felt like to be an adoptee, nor would I expect her to understand. I did want her to have some level of acceptance of the importance of it to me. That was never to be. As I had thought about searching for my birth family many times by the age of twenty-one, there was never a move to action. I was interested in seeing and meeting everybody biologically related to me. I wanted to know more; where my birth family lived, who all was living and had they wondered about me. I wanted to tell my birth mother that I had been fine and my childhood had been a very good one. I wanted to know if my birth mother had wanted to keep me and had it been her decision to create an adoption plan.

I had been led to believe that my birth family wanted the very best for me and didn't think they could provide that. I believed what I was told throughout my childhood. If I had a choice of what to think since the truth was unknown, then I chose a thought that was pleasing to me. It was kinder and gentler to believe that deep down my first family wanted to keep me, but they didn't see how it would work for everybody's good. I had basically the same three questions birth mothers typically have about the baby they relinquished to adoption: Is she still alive? Is she in good health? What sort of life did she have without me? Also, I knew that there was probably not a chance of my birth family finding me, because my name had been changed from the one they had known. Under a closed system, everything seemed designed to keep us apart.

I continued to believe that the opportunity would present itself in the future for a reunion with my birth family while I enjoyed my real and ever-present family. I actually couldn't envision my life being any better under other circumstances, but certainly different. I felt fortunate to be with a family that embraced and loved me as if we were related by blood. It felt good to belong to a group of some of the strongest, vibrant and successful people I knew, like my aunt Annie Lee, who had become an accomplished artist throughout the world. She had achieved a level of success in the art community by being sort of a comedian with a paintbrush. When I would accompany her on art shows, her fans stopped at nothing to show their admiration. Some would cry upon meeting her as they explained how long they had been collecting her art: *Blue Monday, Six No Uptown, 5th Grade Substitute, Al Ain't Here, Gimme Dat Gum, Primpin', E'body Say Amen, Second Set, 8 ½ Narrow, 100% Cotton, Hot Water Cornbread, 60 Pounds,* and on and on and on.

Others would kindly ask for me to take a photo of them with her after making yet another purchase of an original, limited edition, figurine or other art creations by my aunt. I was by her side to assist at several art galleries and events that took me to places all over the country. She allowed me, as her one and only niece, to experience what fame looks like up close and personal. She loved me unconditionally, and I never seemed too far from her wealth of wisdom. I can recall asking her if she wondered about people gravitating to her and being nice because of her success. She responded, "No, I don't know people's motives, but it doesn't matter. I try to treat everyone with kindness and let God handle the rest." That was some powerful advice, and it reminds me to trust God and love people. I could call her at any time, visit at the drop of a hat, and she showered me with immeasurable gifts throughout my life. Most importantly, she made herself available despite her schedule and constantly shared how she was so proud of me. I had her blessings to find my birth family and she was most interested in knowing more of my journey when the time was right.

The fact still remained that I didn't have my mother's blessing to search. I considered how an infertile woman might feel about it. In the 1960s, my mother's friends were getting pregnant and having children. Her friends' friends were having babies. I hoped that she didn't feel inadequate or disempowered as a woman by her inability to conceive a baby. It seemed like the idea that I might find the woman who was able to get pregnant and deliver me into the world was overwhelming to her, and I never wanted to add to her pain. I didn't see her problem as my situation to fix, but I believed I owed it to my mother to honor her wishes about a subject that hurt her to the core. My separation and relinquishment didn't shake my foundation in the way infertility seemed to do her. She wasn't able to be a mother the natural way and resorted to a plan B. The idea of me wanting to reunite with a woman – my first mother – who didn't have to rely on another method of having a child seemed disrespectful to my mother, and yet it was far from that. Perhaps at the time that was the people pleaser in me; often a common trait among adoptees.

The truth about my beginnings would remain far from my grasp for many years, and it certainly didn't help matters that the Illinois adoption law prevented me from obtaining information or leads. Subconsciously, I knew if I had placed a call to someone for help, they would ask, "What was your entire name? Bonnie what? What hospital were you born at? Was it a private adoption or through an agency?" I had no answers to all these and other questions. For me, it simply still wasn't the time in 1985 to learn the truth about about my first chapter.

Adoptive parents tend to be ambivalent about their child's mention of wanting to search for their biological family. My mother couldn't shake the thought that my love for her would change, and that our relationship would change too. I knew without a doubt that it wouldn't change anything for the worse. It would add to me feeling more whole. She also expressed being protective of me. She felt that I might not like what I found after searching for the people biologically related to me.

I wondered what she could possibly mean by that. I never gave much thought to receiving undesirable news about biological family members. All families have dysfunction, dirty laundry, secrets, lies, sickness and death. I was experiencing all of that with my current family. Why would it be any different with my biological family? Not knowing of my birth family was the undesirable news, but my preoccupation with all the other moving parts of my life kept my mind far from a birth family reunion. I was accomplishing things, experiencing places, and enjoying the people already present in my life. That was enough for the time being.

Something else about the 1980s, the idea never occurred to me that I could meet with other adoptees for open discussions about adoption: to go to a place where I could talk openly about anything and everything related to my identity as an adopted person and hear from others in the constellation about their experience. It never dawned on me that having a place to hear and share adoption stories might be deeply beneficial. I don't recall picking up a book about adoption, not even Dr. Seuss's *Are You My Mother?*

Instead, I was starting to find my way through this adoption thing by reading books in the self-help section of the bookstore or library. My mother owned several of these kinds of books and didn't mind me taking a peek inside their covers. Dr. Wayne Dyer was one of the first authors I can remember from my mother's library when I discovered his book *Your Erroneous Zones*. I learned that he too was separated from his birth mother. I also became acquainted with Leo Buscaglia through *Personhood: The Art of Being Fully Human*.

I was starting my path of seeking something far greater than religion seemed to offer me. I was primarily raised in the Lutheran church, and when I first heard the mention of Martin Luther, I wondered about the connection between him and the civil rights leader. The Martin Luther who was excommunicated by the pope in 1521 believed that eternity into heaven is a free gift and cannot be earned through good deeds. Through my upbringing, I memorized all the books of the Old and New Testaments. I had a fairly good knowledge of scripture from the King James version of the Bible. I was more interested in spirituality over religion, but I hadn't a clue that's what I was seeking at the time. My daily routine was focused on what I possessed instead of what was missing from my life.

I continued with my college classes and sought another part-time job closer to the campus. I ducked in and out of downtown Chicago buildings to submit applications before going inside of City Hall. It was about three in the afternoon when people were swarming around to complete a 3X5 index card to apply for the Chicago Police exam. I might as well fill one out, I thought. I left the building and didn't give it a second thought. Over the course of two years while still in school and during the time in 1986 when Dr. King's birthday became a national holiday in only seventeen states, I finished each phase of the Chicago Police Department's pre-academy testing.

Being a police officer was somewhat of a foreign idea to me, and my encouragement mainly came from my father. He believed that I had what it took to handle that kind of career. He had enough belief in me for the both of us. He didn't doubt that the Chicago Police Department would train and prepare me for the job. Most of my friends were not convinced that it was a good choice and tried to discourage me by saying how dangerous it would be for anyone in a place like Chicago. I stood about 5'4" and weighed no more than 125 pounds. It seemed that I was no match for even a one-time encounter with a career criminal. How would I handle some of the most dangerous situations out in the world? It was true; I wasn't street smart. I had been sheltered most of my life from even the drug addicts and alcoholics in my family. I only had an incomplete undergraduate education in the social sciences and hung around friends with similar backgrounds. What did I know? The most important thing I knew is I had the support of my family and a calling to fulfill. If it did not work out or the wheels fell off, I still had to pursue or answer the call.

I was eventually accepted into the family of law enforcement on March 9, 1987 and started an 18-week long police-training program just before my 23rd birthday. My studies at UIC came to a halt for at least one year to give all my attention to being a cop. The naysayers still continued their pleas for me to change my mind, but I would think, If I don't like it, I can just quit. I wasn't a quitter, but I knew I had options. I was creating the opportunity to allow this new challenge to prepare me emotionally and spiritually for a birth family reunion though I did not know it. There comes a time when resistance can signal that you are gaining or advancing towards an important thing. I was young enough, and most of all clear enough about my interests. I loved driving, being outdoors, meeting people and solving mysteries. It was my knowing that I had nothing to lose and everything to gain. The author Joseph Campbell describes the first step in *The Hero's Journey* as the call to adventure. "Once you recognize that feeling and heed that call, your life which is your adventure truly begins." If anything could offer me taking the yellow brick road to meet the scarecrow for a better mind, the tin-man for more heart and the lion for deeper courage as Dorothy did on her travels, it was police work.

4 JOINING THE FAMILY OF LAW ENFORCEMENT

It didn't take long for my perception of the police to change for the better, because now I had a different frame of reference.

With each passing day of learning the ropes of my new career in law enforcement, things made more sense when I kept it simple like the child in this joke.

Larry 's kindergarten class was on a field trip to their local police station where they saw pictures tacked to a bulletin board of the ten most wanted criminals. One of the youngsters pointed to a picture and asked if it really was the photo of a wanted person. "Yes," said the policeman. The detectives want very badly to capture him."

Larry asked, "Why didn't you keep him when you took his picture?"

By the tenth week of the police academy, I had mastered the physical education portion and struggled a bit with the law until it became obvious just how important that part is to the job. I became proficient in firearms and a variety of other courses while wondering all the time where this career was going to take me. By July 1987, I was assigned to the streets of Chicago wearing a light blue short-sleeve police shirt, a nameplate that read GHOSTON, a star with the number 5017, navy slacks, and a two-layered checkerboard band around my hat. I carried a Smith & Wesson .357, handcuffs, cuff keys, a nightstick, a flashlight, and a police radio.

It was the beginning of a ride on the river that proved to be nothing close to the one-hour television police dramas. My first day was uneventful. A few in-progress calls like "a man with a gun," or "a domestic disturbance," but the adrenaline flows regardless of what's really going on at the time. "Exercise caution" could be heard throughout my tour of duty from radio dispatchers when they assigned me to an emergency. I would think, "Isn't caution to be exercised on every call?" Another way to put it was: "I better pay attention out here. I could get killed, I could get hurt, I could get somebody else hurt or killed.

As a police officer, you are hyper-vigilant. I experienced all the signs written about by Kevin M. Gilmartin, Ph.D. who spent twenty years in law enforcement and wrote *"Emotional Survival for Law Enforcement, A Guide for Officers and Their Families"* stated the things I experienced and the signs of "increased peripheral vision, more focused hearing, an increased heart rate – all biological responses that enhance survival." It was clear to me that everyone who saw me knew my position of authority in society, because of the uniform. I had this sense that I was a target, whether people were aiming harm in my direction or not. Officers don't have the luxury of knowing the people they come in contact with or their intentions unless they have had repeated interactions. Overall, I enjoyed the first weeks and months leading up to my new assignment as an officer in uniform. Now, I was among the first emergency responders. It was exciting, enjoyable, and most of all interesting as I learned new ways of arriving at the truth during an investigation. The stress was real. As the police, vicarious traumatic stress was even more real on a daily basis. I was listening to the firsthand traumatic experiences of other people through each interview and interaction.

I was never too fond of police officers before becoming one, because I didn't personally know anyone who had been in the career for any significant amount of time. Most of my encounters with law enforcement had been traffic stops or when my dad reported a car theft. My family specifically limited our contact with the police to keep them out of our business. On one evening before becoming an officer, I was driving too fast for the rainy conditions and got pulled over by a one-man police unit. The officer was indifferent towards me. I received two citations from

him to appear in court before he sent me on my not-so-merry way.
I vowed that the police were best to be avoided and wanted little or
nothing to do with them, and I believed they represented what I
had seen on videos of the 1960 rioting in Chicago.

I didn't know that the same officer writing me those tickets that
day would one day be sitting beside me in a squad car. I asked him
one afternoon as I sat in the passenger's seat, "Do you remember
me?" He glared at me for a couple of seconds and said, "From
where?" I responded, "You wrote me two tickets for speeding a
couple of years ago." His smile revealed that he didn't have a clue.
I said, "Yeah, you stopped me and now we're working together."
We both smiled as I thought, You never know who you'll see
again.

It didn't take long for my perception of the police to change for the
better, because now I had a different frame of reference. My
partners were some of the nicest people you ever want to meet.
They were ordinary and everyday people who simply wanted to do
a good job, so they could then return home to their families at the
end of the tour. Law enforcement officers are members of society.
The personality or attitude of the people in Chicago (or anywhere
else for that matter) is exactly what you get from its police
population. Oftentimes there are good actions, and one too many
times something far less than the best from my brothers and sisters
in blue. The police are my family now, and like relatives, some
make decisions that negatively impact and affect the lives of others.
I'm passionate about the police being held to a higher standard by
the public it serves, and any criminal or official misconduct is
unacceptable. Responsibility and accountability is of the utmost
importance when individuals have the type of authority given to
peace officers.

On November 25, 1987, news spread quickly of Mayor Harold
Washington's death. I thought about all the long hours of
campaigning to get him elected and re-elected into office when I
was an undergraduate student. He suffered a heart attack at the age
of 65, and one 73-year-old supporter, Ollie Hawkins, was quoted in
the New York Times as saying, "When I was young, we never
dreamed there'd be a black mayor of Chicago someday. We're

going to miss Harold."

His loss could be felt throughout the City of Chicago and most definitely in its police department. There were more blacks in specialized units, receiving promotions and rising to top commands than ever before during Washington's four years as mayor. The black officers assigned to the Harold Washington detail on the Chicago Police Department could tell you how a tide had changed with regard to business as usual in a city well known for its political corruption. Washington's death meant things were going to change again, and not necessarily in the interests of black people. As a rookie, I could feel the impact of Washington's death by observing veteran officers. Blacks grieved our loss, while many whites seemed relieved, because they hadn't necessarily benefited on the job with Washington in office like they were accustomed to in past times.

Reeling from the death of a great man and mayor of Chicago, my first year as a police officer consumed me. I had so much going on off-duty that my head was spinning most of the time. I was moving into my first apartment, planning a wedding and forming lasting friendships with those who worked along side of me. As my new family grew with each detail, assignment, and new unit, I quickly developed a sense that I could trust that my fellow officers had my back and I had theirs. Police work had my undivided attention if I was going to go home every night in the same condition as when I had started my day. There were few empty spaces to my weeks and months to give serious thought to a reunion with my birth family. Besides, I needed more information for a searcher or someone willing to help me. Meeting my original family was still on hold until such a time that I got a break in the case. It never occurred to me that my birth family might be looking for me.

As a police officer, I viewed records, documents and official reports to enable me to verify facts about an investigation. The only somewhat unofficial reports during my tours of duty were my nearly illegible notes. They needed to be re-written as soon as possible for an official report that would memorialize the facts as accurately as possible. I had never heard of original information being changed from a report to create a new official document. Except, of course, my amended birth certificate. It was an official report that did not contain the truth in its entirety. Documents of all sorts are the crux of any case, and the truth of those records is imperative to a credible investigation. As a police officer, I used reports within the scope of my job to get a better understanding of the people in question. It is always necessary to have the truthful backstory for piecing current events together. It would take over fifteen years and hundreds of criminal investigations later to draw out of me what finding the truth or not finding it really meant as it related to my birth family.

It did not take long for me in my career to realize that no two people see the same incident in the same way. After a traffic accident viewed by several witnesses, each person gives their own different account of the situation. Studies have shown that a man can enter a room and his description will vary among each person who witnessed him. Even his actions while in a given area will be disputed depending on where observers are seated and their angle or view of him. All of this suggests a quote by Anais Nin, "We see things not as they are, but as we are." I would witness this countless times in my career for many years to come.

I graduated from the police academy on March 9, 1988 after completing a one-year probationary period and just seven months prior to tying the knot and becoming Mrs. Jennifer Dyan Ghoston-Bullock. A medium size wedding attended by family and friends went off without any major glitches on October 1, 1988 as I walked down the aisle to Elton John's "Your Song" followed by a honeymoon in Las Vegas. Being a newlywed and returning to work found me in a good place. I set my sights on returning to school, purchasing a house and learning more about solving cases.

I returned to UIC to complete my undergraduate degree and I was taking it slow with only one class when during the afternoon while on campus, a call from my doctor's office had unexpected news: "Your pregnancy test came back positive. Congratulations." I was totally caught off guard, but excited to know that I was carrying a biological connection of life inside of me. One day this baby snuggled tightly in my womb would meet me face to face. Boy or girl, it didn't matter, and all I needed to do was get ready for this little one's arrival. I considered names: Leah, Lee, Arianna, Hope,

Dawn or Malachi, Malcolm and Victor. I didn't actually know for months to come that Andre Edward Bullock Jr. would be his name. Meanwhile, the state of Illinois was sealing birth records again to ensure that adoptees would never see their OBC and possibly prevent a reunion with their original family.

5 A BIOLOGICAL CONNECTION

There is a connectedness to everything and everybody on one level or another.

I was pretty sure that I had conceived on the first anniversary of my wedding day once I learned of my due date of July 2, 1990. My OBGyn doctor was pregnant too; with twins. She gave me explicit instructions to watch my weight gain. My cravings for fried foods, and all the other wrong stuff won over nearly everyday. I had a happy and healthy nine months thinking of the gift God was entrusting to me. It meant someone possibly looking just like me, having characteristics similar to mine and being my first known blood relative. It was truly an exciting time.

My labor was fourteen hours long, and the first person I knew to be biologically related to me was born on Saturday, June 30, 1990 in the morning. He weighed 8lbs., 4oz. and was seventeen inches long. He was a beautiful baby and I wondered if we would eventually look alike. My blood ran through him and his through mine. I now had a good idea about the rite of passage to motherhood, too. My relationship with him had started nine months before, and we even shared the same blood type (B+). This connection between us was indeed a powerful revelation, and I didn't take it lightly. I understood the gravity of having been allowed to bring a life through me into the world, especially when I had no other connection to anyone else quite like it.

The fact that a relationship starts between a mother and her child during those nine months was very clear to me in an instant. I've been in relationships with people for far less time than that and they have had a lasting impact on me. It became real to me that my birth mother had a relationship with me and I with her that had abruptly come to an end twenty-six years ago after being together for nine months. I don't believe we ever forget that bond formed in the womb. It is a relationship during those months together on an emotional, spiritual and physical level. Words were never spoken to her by me, but I could feel her energy and she mine. Though circumstances, time and space separated us then and now, the bond is everlasting. She was still a part of me through the separation. I knew that now having given birth myself.

Now, I had one biological connection in life and it felt extraordinary. More importantly, as I nurtured my young son, I developed a clear understanding about the choice to love – nurture and nature holding hands again. It just happened that he would receive both from me. Thank God, I made it and had great parents. I thought on many melancholy nights, I have always had a chance at life and love. Some years later, I vowed to remember another quote by Troy Dunn, "blood really isn't thicker than water".

As a wife and mother juggling a career in law enforcement, there just didn't seem to be enough room to add anything else to the mix, but I wanted to know if people I passed on the street were related to me. Chicago, being a big city with over three million people coming and going in different directions, made it a place where things all seemed to be moving at once. Birth family members could be anywhere, but I doubted if they knew me, and I certainly didn't know them.

There was a case in the 1990s while working early in the morning on the west side when I knew that my perception of cases was going to leave a deep impact on my life. I was working undercover with my partner when two cars speeding northbound passed us. I was driving a covert vehicle and took notice of a verbal altercation between drivers in two different cars. I made a U-turn to follow the cars and ended up in front of the Area Four Detective Division at Harrison and Kedzie Avenue. Within an instant, more than one shot was fired inside of one car by an unknown offender seated behind the wheel of the other vehicle. All of this was unfolding within seconds at the front doors of a police station.

Didn't the shooter know where he was and who was watching? The enormous proportion of passion involved in this crime was obvious. What was the backstory of this scene? The driver who had fired shots sped away as I followed directly behind him. My partner gave a description of the gunman over his police radio. Responding units readily identifiable as the police were able to safely stop the shooter in his vehicle, place him into police custody and recover a firearm from him. This case had everything to do with how things can change so quickly when it's least expected. The last thing I was told about the victim in this case is she remained in a vegetative state after being shot in the head by the offender, who believed she had stolen items from him.

Another time early in my career when I learned that things happen so quickly was also on the west side of Chicago. An elderly woman was with a child who appeared to be about two years old. As the child wandered away from the woman, I was driving westbound on Madison Avenue. Something caught the woman's attention and she didn't observe the child run into the busy intersection. I put my squad car in park and jumped out to alert oncoming traffic of the little girl. I grabbed the child and walked her back to the woman. I'd like to think that the average citizen would have done what I did that day, but as the police, it's an automatic response without a thought that it's someone else's job. The police are keenly aware of being ready, willing and able to take action when things change. And things were always changing around me. The question was, "Will I be ready, getting ready, or staying ready for what's next?"

There is a connectedness to everything and everybody on one level or another. It reminds me of years of doing puzzles with my mother as a child. We would start puzzles of 500, 750 or 1000 pieces on a regular basis. We would use a large table in the kitchen, living room or wherever we could find a flat surface to arrange the puzzle pieces and begin our work to finish the picture. It would take us weeks and sometimes months to complete the puzzle, but it was well worth the time. We would talk, laugh, smile and oftentimes be completely dumbfounded about what piece fit where. Even though we had put like pieces together, like the blue sky, green grass, reds, yellows, and browns, it took a while to correctly fit them all into their respective place. Certainly, we were in search of the big picture and how all the pieces fit together, but walking by those puzzles on the table was the journey towards the end. This pastime would prove to be a metaphor for life as it relates to places, things and, above all, people being connected to each other. I was often in search of the bigger picture on and off-duty, especially as it related to death.

A year before my dad's passing on February 28, 1991, Nelson Mandela was released from prison. And though apartheid in South Africa wouldn't occur for another three years at least Mandela wouldn't die behind bars, because of his stand against an unjust government. The month of February was quickly filling up with anniversaries, some better than others. I experienced much reflection throughout a month with the fewest days. My dad's death shook my world, and for a long time when I would think about the events that preceded his death, it never made me feel better.

It was a rare occasion for me to accompany my father to his doctor's appointment, because that was what my mother faithfully did for months. The doctors didn't know why they didn't know why, but they simply didn't know what the hell was ailing my dad. After we left the doctor's office and drove home, Dad said, "I can't get out of the car."

"What do you mean? You can't get out of the car? Do you need me to come around and help you out of the car"? I asked.

Dad said, "No, I can't get out of the car. Just let me sit here a minute."

"Okay," I said.

We sat for about ten minutes in silence with me glancing at Dad every few seconds to observe his closed eyes and shallow breaths.

"Okay. You ready now?" I asked.

"No. Just a few more minutes."

"Dad, do you want me to take you back to the doctor?"

He didn't respond.

"Dad. Are you okay?"

I began to feel anxiety well up in my chest and the full understanding that enough had been said and a move to action was necessary at that very moment.

"Let me take you back to the doctor."

I immediately drove past the doctor's office and to a nearby hospital's ER and got assistance to remove Dad from the car. He was wheeled into the sitting area until he could be seen by a triage nurse. Minutes seemed like hours and I finally got restless and demanded that Dad's vitals be taken. They were unstable and he was rushed into the back to be hooked up to a bunch of machines. I grew more anxious and unsettled about the sudden scurry of the medical staff. I stayed with Dad once the family was allowed in the back and held his hand. That time with him calmed and renewed my spirit. He seemed to be feeling better, and I asked, "How do you feel?"

He nodded his head up and down.

I smiled and said, "Dad, you're going to be fine."

He continued nodding his head and eventually said with a deep sigh, "I'm tired. I'm tired."

The nurse and doctor returned to the room and suggested that I leave while they gave Dad an examination, so I returned to the waiting area with my mother. We sat and kept each other company until further notice.

Two hours later, I looked at my watch and I realized I had almost forgotten to pick up my son from the babysitter. I told Mom that I would return quickly and to call me if she thought of anything for me to bring back to the hospital. I was allowed to go in the back to tell Dad that I would be right back. He smiled and shook his head up and down as I left the room. As I drove from the parking lot, thoughts of the morning and afternoon made me sure a change was near. In one direction, I was thinking about my dad, and in reverse, my mind was on my nearly one-year-old son.

I placed Andre in the car seat and headed back to the hospital. I received a phone call from Mom saying that I needed to hurry back to the hospital and meet her in the chaplain's office. I should have known what that meant from my police experience, but it did not register with me at that time. Upon my arrival to the waiting area with my son in my arms, Mom was not in the room. I quickly located the quiet room down the corridor on the left and found my mother seated in silence with watery eyes. Catholic hospitals are not short on staff to greet you in times of sadness and grief, so the nun in the room smiled while ushering me to take a seat between the chaplain and Mom. I held my bright-eyed son and called my husband on the phone to bring him up to speed on the situation. In my four years of police experience, I had met with families for the purpose of notifying them of tragedies in rooms like this. I had even conducted interviews in hospitals like this when people had just experienced a death, but I had never been sitting in this seat while my Dad or anyone as close to me lay in a back room being "tired." I no longer throw around that word.

"Your loved one is not doing so well, so we wanted to meet with you. Pray with you," the chaplain softly spoke.

"Can I go see him now?"

"Let us pray," he said.

We bowed our heads.

The chaplain finally answered my request: "You may see your dad now."

As I prepared to walk with the chaplain down the hall, a doctor entered the room with his head down. He said, to my mother, "Your husband's heart has stopped beating."

"What?" I asked.

I couldn't believe it! I didn't know what to do. I said, "Can we see him?"

What remained in that cold room on that very sad afternoon was the flesh my dad had occupied for seventy-five years. I went over to him and cried tears that just wouldn't stop.

I needed a cigarette badly. I stood over my dad's remains, said a prayer, and vowed that he would be with me forever. I had no clue at the time what that really meant. I returned to the quiet room and held my son and hugged my mother. We cried for what seemed like hours before we left the hospital. We were all changed by this event, and I was convinced that I needed answers. Phone calls to his doctor provided no closure, and I suggested that we decline an autopsy. I had seen dozens of them at work and the thought of my dad being cut in that manner repulsed me. Mom agreed and we set into motion a proper funeral and burial service for my father. I smoked a cigarette after the private viewing of Dad's body at the funeral home and wondered why the makeup had to be caked on his face. I guess I understood the preparation, but I didn't like it. Sometimes you just have to accept things if you can't appreciate, enjoy or be enthusiastic about them.

The month of May brings flowers after April's showers, but I was in a dark place that spring, unable to appreciate my good life. The thought of my parents being old enough to be my grandparents occupied my thoughts, because my dad was gone. Them leaving me as grandparents sometimes do before your own children are grown and have children seemed like a reasonable possibility, but it didn't feel good.

On May 12, 1991, I was twenty-seven and my son was preparing to have his first birthday when there it was in the Chicago Sun-Times: "Adopted – and on a mission." If I searched for my birth family and found my parents, then I would have a crack at still having parents in the next forty, fifty, sixty years. The reasons for reuniting with my birth family continued to increase, or at least I kept thinking of why it was important. I was close to the age of the black woman in the article who had begun a search for her birth mother. She was born at Michael Reese Hospital in Chicago and weighed two pounds. She was placed in foster care after her mother disappeared in 1958. By 1960 she was adopted by a married couple. Her story went on to say, "My parents have been great. I'm not looking for a new family or more love. I am looking for answers in the missing pieces of my life so, I can have a whole life and be a complete person."

Her story intrigued me. She found her birth mother in New York City and listened on the phone as her husband talked to the woman on the other end.

"Do you know anyone named Jane?"

The woman responded, "No, but I had a daughter."

This adoptee had been acknowledged by her birth mother and said, "I felt completeness, relief from all the frustration, confusion and whatever else I felt during the years."

Along the right side of page three of that article was another one, "A difficult time for adoptive parents," by Leslie Baldacci. It asked the question, "What about parents who have raised adopted children, then must stand back during the search for the biological mother?"

Why wouldn't parents be standing with the adoptee during a time that we just want to know where we come from? Still another article on the same page in the lower left hand corner read, "Some want records shut." Judge Joseph Schneider, presiding judge of the county division of Cook County Circuit Court said he had heard from a birth mother who pleaded that her secret never be revealed. "Her husband did not know she had a child before their marriage. It would destroy her, and their marriage, if he found out." He heard from an adoptee who lived in fear that someone would knock on her door and announce, 'I am your mother. I would not want my records to be made available.'

What did all three of these articles reveal to me? When reading them, I was now ambivalent about whether a search and reunion was a good idea. I wasn't the least bit concerned about ruffling anyone's feathers especially if I was still a secret. On a few occasions, I thought that my birth family's rejection of me in 1964 meant "shame on you", but if I encountered rejection a second time as a result of my search, "shame on me." Why put myself in that vulnerable position to be rejected again? But then again why not take the chance that I would be accepted by my first family? Those thoughts about rejection never got a stronghold in my mind, because of my belief that good decisions had been made in the past with all concerned parties. I would do my part to find my birth family in time.

Four years later, in 1995, when I was bathing my son, I suspected that he had contracted the chicken pox virus when I noticed blisters on his body. I thought nothing more than to care for him. I bathed him in Aveeno and within less than forty-eight hours, I began to feel extremely ill. I ran a high fever as large and small blisters formed on nearly every inch of my body. My arms, legs, face, hands, lips and every open cavity of my being were covered with the effects of the outbreak. I had contracted a full-blown case of the chicken pox from my son and couldn't recall ever being that sick. I had been infected in the worst way and was off work for weeks. The CPD didn't want me anywhere near other members, because it could potentially bring the department to its knees. It was far worse than my labor and giving birth. As the weeks passed and my health improved, I knew that this maddening situation was simply a test of a mother's love. I sometimes thought that I would have stayed as far away from my son as possible during his bout with the virus if I had known of the consequences. On second thought, we were connected like two puzzle pieces and I wouldn't have changed a thing, because he was my son and I his mother.

Once my health and that of my son's was restored, he was back to his routine and I was back to mine, solving cases.

1996 ushered in a changing me and only time would tell if it was for the best. I lost considerable weight due to having braces in my mouth for a year and my marriage was moving towards its end. A separation led Andre and I to live with my mother for a short time while the ink was preparing to dry on divorce papers. I reluctantly returned to the house where there was once three family members and began occupying the same space with just the two of us. Somewhere in the world, my birth family was doing their own thing; living their lives. Were they happy? Did they think of me? Had they considered a reunion with another member of their family that they had never gotten to know? Whatever answers were held for those questions, my immediate family was rearranging its pieces. Fortunately, it wasn't a bitter breakup and often referred to in court documents as irreconcilable differences. My son and I found righteous contentment in being together and creating a new normal. On one evening as we watched television, we did not know that I would be conducting an off-duty investigation as he looked on and just as unsure as me of what was going to unfold before our eyes.

We watched the pouring rain through the picture window in our living room. I observed a small child standing on the porch of a house directly across the street. She appeared to be about two years old. I told a young Andre to watch from the window as I left my home to check on this little person. As I approached her, the rain was a steady downpour. She was leery, but gave me her attention with big brown eyes. I repeatedly rang the doorbell of the house and received no response. I asked her, "Where's your mommy?" She said nothing. I pointed to my house where she could see Andre looking through the window at us and I suggested that she come in out of the rain. She agreed and took my hand. She entered my home and remained at the big picture window looking outside for someone to return for her.

The child remained at my house for over an hour standing at the window and occasionally going to a nearby cocktail table, but never losing sight of the outdoors where someone had left her. I wondered just what to do and who would leave her like this. I had fleeting thoughts of adopting her. She needed a good home and I could provide that. She needed a levelheaded and sensible mother, and I qualified there too. And just like that, the little girl observed a woman exit a house next door to the one she had been in front of when I first saw her. She immediately ran to my front door to be reunited with a woman walking towards a car. I walked with the child in the downpour to this unknown woman. She ran with relief to the woman and I proceeded to initiate a conversation about this little girl being left alone.

The woman explained to me that she had left her sleeping two-year old daughter in the car while she attended a meeting at my neighbor's home. She thought the child would remain asleep throughout her visit and didn't anticipate any problems. I returned to my home thinking about that mother. Should I be placing a call to the Department of Children and Family Services (DCFS)? Was it in order to report this mother to someone? My unsettled feelings subsided over the next couple of days and my career would quickly prove that just when I thought I had seen it all, that was far from the truth.

6 DISCOVERING THE TRUTH OR NOT

Some investigations lasted weeks, others months and more lasted years before learning the truth.

I was promoted to detective with the Chicago Police Department during the fall of 1998 after being a police officer for over eleven years. I was thirty-four years old. Just one month prior to my promotion, I wrote in my journal on 13 October 1998 in the A.M. the following:

"My dog is expected to live for about 6 months to a year. She has 'Degenerative Myelopathy'. Her spinal condition is paralyzing her body. She now drags her hind legs. She's 7 years old. I always thought she would at least be around for another 5-10 years."

It was time to say goodbye to a most beautiful and gentle German Shepherd named Felony. I was no stranger to separation and loss, so I remained thankful for the time however long or short spent with her. I was thankful too for every other thing in my life. I hadn't a clue at the time that just fourteen days later, I would receive the most exciting and happiest news.

I wrote in my journal in 1998 about my appointment to detective. I could not believe it. I was totally shocked by the news. I was overwhelmed, excited and very much looking forward to what this assignment really meant. I knew that my name had been submitted for a meritorious promotion, but I hadn't really thought that I would be chosen out of the many qualified candidates being considered for this honor. The idea of actually working in the Investigative Bureau of the Detective Division for the Chicago Police Department took more than a few days to completely process. I just remember reporting to the police academy to give a urine sample and being briefed on the training to start at Malcolm X College.

I completed detective training, graduated and welcomed the opportunity to apply myself in this new field. My first day at Area Two did not disappoint, because I was assigned to the violent crimes unit on the second watch. I was fully ready to do a good job.

All I had ever wanted to be was a detective since coming on the police department in 1987. Trading in the role of a preliminary investigator for one as a detective meant being held accountable for everything on any given investigation. It was my first major assignment after my promotion to assist experienced detectives on the homicide of a police officer, John Knight. My responsibilities included, but certainly were not limited to, canvassing the neighborhood for possible witnesses and obtaining evidence to help solve the case. I rang doorbells and knocked on doors in search of anyone who may have seen or heard what happened in the community on that morning and early afternoon.

Knight had been gunned down about a mile from my home on the south side. He had been working as a plainclothes tactical officer when he and his partner placed a stop on two young men. Before Knight could exit his squad car, one gunman repeatedly fired on him, causing his death. It was one of the coldest days so far that winter in Chicago as I worked the neighborhood, and learned at least two important things that day: carry pencils, so I could continue writing in the cold when the ink froze in my black pens, and to trade my six-shot revolver for a Smith & Wesson model 669, a thirteen-shot, double-action, semi-automatic weapon in the name of being prepared and ready for whatever might happen. That's what police really get paid for: what might happen while you're working the streets.

The gunman had used an automatic weapon that he emptied and reloaded in a matter of seconds on Knight. And though Knight's murder was solved within twenty-four hours, I soon learned that many a mystery lasts a whole lot longer. Not unlike my original identity and that of my first family.

By New Year's Day 1999, the cold temperatures dipped even further into the single digits and I had no use for a pen to take notes outdoors. It was about twelve in the afternoon when my two partners and I were the lead detectives on a homicide. Upon arrival on the scene, we discovered the body of a man slouched over the driver's seat of a four-door vehicle. His elderly passenger was still on the scene and refused to tell us the truth. There was contraband in the car and rumors of a second passenger who was nowhere to be found.

Sometimes you know something about what happened, but that's simply not enough evidence. We worked for months and ultimately years on that case. The meaning of "taking it to your grave" rang loudly for me night after night for weeks about this investigation. The elderly witness in the case took most of his knowledge of the incident to his grave when I learned of his death from an illness a few years later. As the months of my career went by, I added another measure of investigative success to the pot: accept that there will be things you may never know, and there will be even more things that you don't know that you don't know. It was during this time that my mother's health was in its second year of decline.

My mother had been diagnosed with cancer and had surgery to remove a tumor the size of a grapefruit from her colon. She received a colostomy bag after a large section of her colon was removed to prevent an infection. I knew that I would have to change the bag for her, because she couldn't even bear to look at this new opening on the side of her body. After about three months, when I made my usual visit in the morning to her home, she said, "Come in here. I want to show you something." I entered her bedroom, and she motioned for me to come closer to her. She pointed to her side and said, "Look." I saw a clean colostomy bag hanging from her mid-section. She had found the courage to change it herself. We smiled, laughed and hugged with joy over a proud moment as mother and daughter sometimes do, knowing all the while that if she had never been able to change her colostomy bag, I would have gladly been able to take care of it. She was my mother, and that would never change. We spent that day and the next three years doing things we might not have done if I had not been struggling with the fact of her mortality.

One of the most important things that my father's death allowed me to do was have a stronger relationship with my mother. After his passing, I naturally drew closer to her by spending more time and seeing to her needs. I can recall being so glad that I only lived one mile from my mother, so it was easy to get back and forth to her home from mine. We did more things together and bonded like never before. The idea of death can really help you to fully live. By this time, I had some timeless principles under my belt and none of it conflicted with my Christian upbringing; instead, it added to it. I had now been reading material from some of the greatest spiritual teachers like Khalil Gibran, Deepak Chopra, and Thomas Moore. It would be another decade before I further learned from other authors like Gary Zukav, Louise Hay, Richard Carlson, Debbie Ford, Iyanla Vanzant, Michael Bernard Beckwith, Don Miguel Ruiz, Esther Hicks and many more. It was also during this time that I began to really appreciate some of our four-legged companions.

I grew up with dogs and some were simply strays that my mother allowed me to feed in our yard, nurture back to health and send back out into the world. Valentine was my first mutt during the 1980s who often jumped in bed with me and left her dog hair everywhere. Nevertheless, I loved her dearly. Later would come Misty who was by all accounts my mother's doggie, but I loved her just as much. But, in 1999 after Felony made her transition, Spirit was adopted from a co-worker. While buying a collar for her at a suburban pet store, my nine-year old son looked at an adorable female Rottweiler puppy and asked, "Can we get her and name her Soul?" How could I resist, so I said, "Yes" knowing all the while that I would be taking care of not one dog, but two together for the first time. Spirit had a Soul, and Soul had a Spirit. They were the best company to us and each other. They earned their keep by keeping mischievous people off our property. My love for dogs grew with each passing year and I couldn't imagine ever being without these kinds of family members. I thank my mother for instilling in me the love for animals and adopting dogs. She never gave it a second thought about providing a home to man's best friend.

My mother truly enjoyed being a grandmother and passed her love for doing puzzles to my son, Andre. They would enjoy each other for a total of eleven years after my dad's passing, and we experienced some of the most joyous occasions one can only hope for with a diagnosis of cancer. We began taking full advantage of what living in Chicago meant once she received the news of colon cancer that had metastasized to other parts of her body.

On October 11, 2000, I had two tickets to an Oprah Winfrey Show taping in Chicago about parenting pre-teens, and Mom joined me though she wasn't a fan. When Oprah invited the audience to ask questions, my mother wasn't the least bit shy, and her hand flew way up in the air. Producers of the show had already forewarned us about not asking Oprah for autographs and pictures, because it was too many people for her to accommodate all of us. I was certain that wasn't my mother's inquiry.

Before I could begin to imagine my mother's question, she asked it: "How do I get a copy of your very first O Magazine for my daughter (pointing at me) who loves you? I've given her a subscription to it, but I could never find the very first issue."

Oprah explained to my mother and the audience why she had limited the reproduction of issues, because she couldn't predict the success of the new magazine. Oprah then did something that I absolutely wouldn't have imagined in 1000 years. She directed one of her producers to go to her office and there he would find a copy of the very first O Magazine. He returned with it and handed it to Oprah. She proceeded to ask my mother's name so she could autograph it to her: "Clarice, Many Blessings for Your Best Life, Oprah Winfrey."

By the end of the day, needless to say, Oprah had a new fan in my mother. I, on the other hand, had my sights on seeing Oprah's mentor in person for the first time.

My mother and I went to see and hear Dr. Maya Angelou speak to a crowd of over 2000 people at the university I had attended for my graduate studies. How did Dr. Angelou know that my mother was a librarian when she gave her speech? What splendid wisdom, Dr. Angelou. It seemed like you were speaking directly to my mother about her forty-year career in the Chicago Public High School library. Ms. Angelou stated to a room of us, "Get to know the librarian at your school."

It was as if she was personally valuing and validating my mother's chosen profession as she sat near the front of the stage. Ms. Angelou sang, spoke words of wisdom and sang some more. She sounded beautiful and it was a wonderful time. Maya Angelou stated that she didn't stand alone on that stage. She said, "I come as one, but I stand as 10,000," referring to all the ancestors who came before her and who had paved the way. When I thought that the moments couldn't get any better that year for my mom and I, we celebrated her best and only surprise birthday party – her 77th – on August 11, 2001, and the front of the invitation read:

"Expect a Miracle...and Receive it"

It was during the planning of that party that I realized that my mother had her family, immediate girlfriends, neighbors, church members and co-workers, most of whom had never met each other before that day. Her life brought so many people together and it was demonstrated that evening with a grand celebration of her life. I too bring people together, and that's just one more thing about my adoption that I honor and had in common with my mother. Everyone at the party embraced and honored life's preciousness.

It was during that same year, in August and September that I was a part of a team interviewing over a dozen young women who had each been taken at gunpoint by two or three men. They had each been forced into an alley, backyard or a dark secluded area and sexually assaulted by the same unknown rapists. A reporter for one of the Chicago newspapers, Dan Rozek, correctly stated, "The men usually approach a lone woman, talk to her briefly, then one man displays a handgun and orders her to a vacant lot or secluded area, where she is assaulted and robbed."

We worked on these cases for months before we received the

break we needed one afternoon. A young woman attacked and raped by two men was robbed of her cell phone. Once we were able to obtain numbers made on that phone, we met a person who gave us more leads. After many meetings, interviews, videotaped confessions, recovered stolen items, tears shed by the survivors, sleepless nights, felony charges against three young men were approved by the Cook County State's Attorney's Office. I was convinced that I was becoming a skilled detective by attending to details, being very observant, and most of all, patient.

Just three days later, the U.S. experienced epic terrorism. I wrote in my journal on September 11, 2001: "The World Trade Center was destroyed and over 10,000 people were killed this morning. Four American aircraft were hijacked and tragedies followed quite quickly."

My mother and I were each at our own homes when we learned of the news on television. I called her by phone and we watched in disbelief as reporters spoke of what was unfolding in the sky. The video showed planes crashing into two New York City skyscrapers. It seemed like it couldn't be true, but it most certainly was the truth. My mother had a doctor's appointment that she insisted on keeping, but as I suspected, we were turned away due to the tragedies going on in the country. It would be weeks before we started to process just what terrorism means and what happened that day. "The power of the terrorists is much greater in things that never come to be than it ever is in the things that do come to be."[9] The idea of terrorism or terrorist acts has many people living in a state of fear.

It was almost a year later after solving the case of the bus stop rapists and the horrific news of 9/11 that I received the news from Dr. Qaudir at Little Company Of Mary Hospital of my mom's death on June 11, 2002, at 3:20 P.M. She had suffered a seizure without me by her side. This would be my second parent to die at the same hospital under the same circumstances of me en route to being back at their side. I arrived at the hospital shortly before four in the afternoon and kissed her forehead. I held her hand and told her, "I love you, Mom."

By the time I turned thirty-eight and one month after my mother's
death while going through her things, there were only three
documents to be found relative to my adoption. An envelope from
the law offices of Graham, Stevenson & Griffith contained a letter
dated July 13, 1967. It reads as follows:

Dear Mr. & Mrs. Ghoston:

We are happy to enclose the new birth certificate for your
daughter, Jennifer. Since this brings the matter to a conclusion, we
would like to extend our best wishes to you and your family.

Very truly yours
Graham, Stevenson & Griffith

The same law office sent another notice dated September 1, 1967
that stated that the fee and court cost totaled $90. Another
document was dated June 16, 1966 and it requested that my parents
have medical forms completed for me by a physician. Upon
reading this letter from over four decades before, I realized that my
mother had never shared this information with me in fear that I
might have been able to gain some knowledge about my
beginnings.

Much like a criminal investigation with no leads, my adoption case
remained forever open and pending before moving towards some
truth. I needed more documentation, a witness, something or
someone that would lead me in the direction of what pertains to
me during the first two years of my life. I still had nothing more
than the first name of "Bonnie" given to me at birth. I needed
more information, and just like with most cases, it just takes the
passage of time to arrive at what really happened when those that
know won't tell you.

The starting point is today and yesterday is simply "what could
have happened" had I remained with my original family. The
shoulda, woulda, coulda game as children, teenagers and young
adults is at best fun before it becomes pointless. I don't really know
what the past would look like if it were different than it is. The Law

of Averages or the Law of Attraction suggest that I would likely have lived a very different life if my original family looked very different than my adoptive one. It's not just the physical attributes shared that are a huge factor in remembering and knowing your birth ties, but also in a spiritual connection that I couldn't deny feeling most of the time. There were so many more things to learn from my career and in the emotional preparation for finding the truth in my personal life. I went back to the basics, reading books that suggested a Wayne Dyer quote, "If you change the way you look at things, the things you look at change".

By 2003, I had a calm assurance and acceptance of my mother's transition being a part of life, because I no longer feared the death experience. I had by now seen it too many times in my career and personal life. Death had caused me to understand through the study of it that things may be discovered for great purpose of adding more peace to the in-living-color picture of life, and there may be a need for an extra investigation to arrive at more truth. This was the case one Sunday morning when the sun was shining brightly and it seemed like a wonderful afternoon in the lovely month of May.

I wasn't the least bit interested in a cigarette, because I quit smoking two years prior. I was sitting at a desk in my office thinking about the amount of work overwhelming me. I wasn't behind, but not exactly caught up either. As detectives, there is a tremendous amount of follow-up work. Some investigations never seem to die, especially deaths. There are the countless interviews, the arrests, sifting through the lies, the truth, felony charges, prosecution, subpoenas and court appearances. It is so not like the one-hour TV dramas that people love to watch each week. For every hour spent on the street, at least two, three, four or more hours are spent typing up accurate reports. As I sat there looking through all the reports assigned to me, I looked over at my partners and asked, "So what's up for the day?"

The senior partner of our three-man car said, "Well, a job just came in from the third district. It sounds like a madhouse with the media. Let's head out."

Here we go, I thought.

As we approached the furthest parking lot from our point of interest, every local network was in sight. It was a media frenzy for sure and they were there for the duration. We had seen that before, and knew it was to be expected when tragedy strikes and things are quiet elsewhere in a big city like Chicago. We parked next to the fire engines and ambulances to walk in together. We entered the building and were quickly directed to the reason we were there. The security officer said, "Detectives, come with me."

He led us through doors restricted to the public and around corners with yellow tape. There were people everywhere in tears, shock and panic. An area roped off with red tape contained the lifeless body of our fifteen-year-old victim. Her skull was cracked and a pool of blood surrounded her. I could hear crying as I scribbled notes of her position on the floor, the lighting in the room and the nearby exhibit. I met with other police personnel and took their names for my reports. I gathered witnesses and as much information as possible to put the pieces together of what led to this tragedy. The paramedics gathered their equipment and left the scene while the remaining emergency responders from the Chicago Fire Department gathered together in another room. Grief counselors were made available for the several hundred students from all over the city and country in the museum that day. In seventy years, it was the first fatality at the Museum of Science and Industry.

We spoke with the teenagers and friends of the deceased who were in the vicinity of her fall from the fourth floor. Their statements were all consistent with pleading with the victim to get down from the railing before something terrible happened to her. The nuns from an out-of-town Catholic high school had taken a rather large group on a field trip to this great city for the weekend. It was supposed to be a good time spent hundreds of miles from home. Instead, it would likely be a life-long memory in the minds of young people with decades of life yet to live. As I spoke at length to dozens upon dozens of strangers of all ages, it was clearly a sad occasion for so many people all at once. I didn't have the task of speaking with the victim's family, so I can only imagine that experience. What I did have the responsibility of that day was putting the death of such a young person in perspective for the purpose of carrying with me the idea of life's uncertainty.

It was Mother's Day when someone's daughter made her transition. I could only imagine as she fell to her death near the pendulum exhibit at the museum witnessed by many other people some much younger than her, just how many lives would forever be touched that day by tragedy. How do you tell a mother of a death investigation concerning her daughter? How do you tell a mother of her son's death to gun violence? That was what my first cousin learned of her oldest son on September 21st of that same year.

That news, I can only imagine changes a mother's life in ways she may never be able to fully articulate and is indeed a life-defining moment for the entire family. My cousin made his transition two months shy of his 30th birthday and his grandmother; my beloved aunt wrote on his obituary, "You were my first grandson…words cannot express my love for you. I will never forget you in my mind, soul and heart."

My return to an office full of work with many other cases seemed to rush in the new year of 2004. The one thing about being busy is time seems to move faster than normal. But, when the call from a family member to give me more news about the death of another first cousin's son, time seemed to come to a complete stop. Another cousin made his transition on March 24th at twenty-nine years old. My aunt; his grandmother again had words for another grandson, "…you were the love of my life and will always be in my heart. I will always love you. I'll miss those big hugs and kisses." She had now buried two grandsons who hadn't seen a complete three decades of their lives and it seemed so unnatural for the older generation to outlive the younger one. We cannot predict the brevity or longevity of a person's life.

That same year, I learned that DNA proved to be the answer to many unanswered questions once the Illinois State Police Criminal Sexual Assault kit and a rapist were linked in CODIS (the Combined DNA Index System). One case took me back to a time before my CPD promotion as detective when, according to reports, a rapist sexually assaulted a teenager on Chicago's south side. In the early part of 1998, a fifteen-year-old girl was walking down the street slightly ahead of her mother and two younger sisters en route home just after sunset. She rounded the corner of her block and out of the sight of her family. According to her, she was then attacked by a man. He grabbed her and took her into a secluded backyard on the same block and raped her. The horrible event happened so fast that she would later tell me in an interview that she tried to pretend it wasn't real.

DNA evidence was introduced at that time as the 21st century miracle investigative tool for criminal investigations. That case was linked to at least four more reported cases that were solved through DNA evidence and victim identifications. A man confessed to the crimes and even admitted to cases that had gone unreported during a ten-year period. Again, I have evidence to support that the truth is often buried, forgotten or simply unknown by those seeking it, sometimes for years and years. Also, it greatly increased my knowledge about how DNA can help the adoption community.

Family Tree DNA, founded in 2000, is only as valuable as the size of the database, but it is an additional resource in discovering one's biological ancestry. FT DNA states, "The larger the database, the more information we can provide you. FT DNA can follow the deep origins of specific family lines (Y-DNA & mtDNA)." [10] 23 and Me is another resource increasingly used by the adoption community in hopes of connecting with one's birth family. The painless process of swabbing your cheek as a part of the DNA kit reminded me of how those of us in law enforcement regularly collect evidence from a suspect in furtherance of an investigation to lead us in the right direction. The collection of DNA can include as well as exclude a person's involvement in a crime and proved to be one of my best resources to move closer to the truth.

The 21st century caught me investigating and solving dozens of high profile sexual assault cases involving serial rapists. Some investigations lasted weeks, others months, and more lasted years. I found myself named in newspaper articles, on camera interviews, making talk show appearances, and part of a Bill Kurtis *Cold Case Files* documentary related to the solving of sexual assaults. I received criticism from the media at times for my beliefs about not allowing your attacker to take you from point A to point B when possible, but most memorable was the kindness shown by a variety of agencies. Many organizations were observant and appreciative of my efforts in the community. There was a long list of men on independent investigations charged with raping young women during the first half of my career in the Detective Division. They eventually pled or were found guilty in a court of law and sentenced to many years in prison.

Through each tedious case, I learned many different things, but mostly I became vigilant in hearing, listening and understanding people from all walks of life with each interview. I learned to ask questions that lead to answers and then more questions. Perhaps most importantly, I discovered that time is often my best friend and allows for the opportunity that a move into action on any subject will present itself. The moment will arrive when more information will be revealed and movement forward towards unanswered questions will in time be the order of the day.

During the fall of 2005, a young man allegedly murdered members of his family. He was accused of stabbing his mother, grandmother and an uncle to death and attempted to kill his sister with a knife after demanding money from them. I assisted on the triple homicide and attempted murder. It brought me face to face with a suspect during the evening of the crime. As he sat in a chair not two feet from me, he repeatedly denied his involvement in the deaths of three of his family members. He was released at that time, because we hadn't yet recovered a video from a store near where the murders took place. A camera had captured him taking off a bloodstained t-shirt and purchasing a new one minutes after the murders in an apartment just blocks away. After physical evidence and witness statements linked him to the murders, I again learned that some things are nearly impossible to believe and accept, though they are entirely true.

As a more seasoned young detective, I had worked on hundreds of investigations that either involved murder, great bodily harm or the

"Aggravated Criminal Sexual Assault," which proved to be where my deep attention to the subject yielded much success. Still, I had given little attention to an investigation closest to my heart: what had happened four decades ago with my original family? Were they still alive? What had their lives been like? What would my beginnings say about my life now? One thing for sure was that over time, the focus and attention to a subject results in many answered questions.

It was in February 2007 when my new partner was assigned to a case of statutory rape that brought me up close and personal with the subject of relinquishment. A thirteen-year-old girl who became pregnant by a man was forced to give up her baby. The young mother relinquished her newborn to an adoption agency upon the insistence of her mother. The baby was born just before the springtime and was likely immediately placed with a new family. It was clear to me just how many entities are involved before, during and after an adoption plan. Hopefully truthful information is maintained in a permanent file, because that adoptee will one day be an adult like me seeking answers. I had no way of determining the number of agencies, institutions, organizations and individuals involved in my adoption story. I already counted over a dozen known sources that might aid in helping me better understand the beginning of my life.

By 2008, Nashville, Tennessee appeared to be calling my name as a possible place to relocate once I reached retirement in a few years. I heard that it was the first southern city to desegregate public establishments after a series of sit-ins by college students in the 1960s. Also, a friend had recommended it to me when I told him that I was looking for a slower pace, a cheaper cost of living, a better winter season and to be close to Chicago. Once I experienced it for myself, I agreed with him. The city offered not too much and not too little of everything that I appreciate.

I traveled back and forth from Chicago to Nashville for over a year during my vacation time and carried on a love affair with the Music City. It was about 450 miles from home and an easy breezy ride south of the Midwest. It was during these rides when I traveled alone that I reflected on my birth family and a reunion. I would imagine asking tons of questions, sharing my life story, viewing pictures from special occasions enjoyed by extended family members and getting caught up with events that happened over the past forty years. I envisioned meeting siblings, aunts, uncles, cousins, nieces, nephews and family friends. The seven hours on the highway allowed for much thought about my separation from however many people were in my bloodline.

On January 7, 2008, I got the call that a third tragic death had occurred in the family. This young cousin had not preceded his grandmother in death, but his mother's words in memory of him, I won't ever forget, "…I can't find the words that would express how I feel other than my love for you will forever transcend all space and time." Again, a mother's loss of her child is difficult if not impossible to express in words.

I immediately joined Mt. Zion Baptist Church in Nashville when Bishop Joseph Walker III said, "If you're traveling back and forth to this city, then you need a covering. Let Mt. Zion cover you." I attended as often as possible and made sure on one particular New Year's Eve, I was seated on a pew among other members. The message that night, "No luggage, no Limit," reassured me that 2009 promised to be bright and prosperous. I had already started my deep study into the Law of Attraction. I really didn't find discrepancies between my solid faith in God and other spiritual teachings. I repeatedly discovered similarities. My participation in Oprah and Eckhart Tolle's *A New Earth* web class discussion was life changing for the better. I discovered more clarity about my journey and how to be more fully present in each moment. I had already read Tolle's *The Power of Now* and understood the basis of his teachings.

With each non-religious spiritual teacher, I focused on the threads between their words and Christianity. Between studying New-Age thought and traveling to other parts of the world, my perception of life was taking on a new beginning. The floodgates opened for me after reading James Allen's book *As A Man Thinketh* to read more books like that one. I explored the metaphysical and spirituality sections on a regular basis in many bookstores. I wanted to discover the possibility of changing my perception about every single thing of the past in a way that best serves me.

I joined a friend in attending my first "Celebrate Your Life" conference near Chicago. Dozens of the authors and spiritual teachers I had come to know through their books and teachings were in attendance. The weekend was one of the best times of my life and I could feel my expansion as a part of the universe. I started experimenting with being able to take my thoughts seriously and as a result become a powerful creator. I recalled the Bible saying that God gave man dominion over the earth.

I started a daily practice of being intentional with my thinking as it related to people, places and things. I removed all the art from the walls of my home that reflected any mood that didn't reflect what I wanted to feel. I replaced them with pictures of couples, or groups of happy people or situations. I started listening to music that uplifted me and reflected love instead of lost love. I nearly had to cease listening to my favorites for a while by Marvin Gaye, Smokey Robinson and Al Green. I'm just kidding, but I was grateful for more uplifting songs like, "Love and Happiness," "Cruisin" and "Let's Get It On." I entertained only the idea of improving all of my relationships with family and friends by extending myself regardless of what they were doing for me. I raised my vibration, and evidence of my success started popping up everywhere.

It was a sunny day on September 12, 2009 when I attracted a man that I started calling my "fly guy" just two months into our relationship. He gave me butterflies. When I thought about him, it felt good with a bit of anxiety, like just before standing up in front of an audience to give an important speech. David was intelligent, funny, handsome and kind. I was on my fourth day of the Master Cleanse and found it interesting that I had been reading from the Book of Psalms as a part of my ten-day fast. The Psalms were written by King David.

At the turn of six months in our relationship, I had met David's mother, son, daughter, and had allowed him to meet my son. We took a road trip to Mississippi, visited two other states, and had some great times together in a short period of time. We did more in a few months than I had ever experienced in any other relationship. Even though I grew weary of traveling over fifty miles one way to his home in Libertyville, Illinois, and my car was starting to make funny noises, it was still worth it. Then one day, while I visited with him, I knew that I was going through a serious shift in what was important to me as an adoptee.

Maya Angelou's quote rang true for me: "At the end of the day, people won't remember what you said or did, they will remember how you made them feel." In general conversation, I heard my "fly guy" loud and clear when he said something like, "Adopted people have serious problems." I didn't know whether to defend myself or ask him to explain. I also realized like never before that there are other people who likely share his opinion. At that point in my relationship with him, I had not discussed being an adopted person and this comment hit my core; a direct assault against adoptees. It didn't seem like a good time to mention that I was that person he thought had problems because of my adoption. Perhaps, I felt he would reject me, or worse, relinquish me. Did I have problems like those identified in the definition of Adopted Child Syndrome or not?

I held my secret until a few days later when the subject came up again and he made a similar statement about adopted people. I couldn't hold it any longer, so I said it. "I was adopted." He looked at me with a hint of embarrassment and I felt total relief about my confession. In that second, I validated myself as an adoptee with problems like everybody else, but not necessarily because of my adoption, or directly related to my being relinquished at birth. We bounced back from that conversation, but it bothered me. I began down the road of more self discovery to see had I missed something about my identity as an adoptee.

I lit a menthol cigarette after being smoke-free for ten years and took a long drag. I was willing to gain clarity about my journey so far. I was interested in taking a serious look at events over the past forty-plus years that accounted for my life experience. It was true that I had ended romantic relationships whenever I suspected the onset of rejection. Was that possibly linked to being relinquished at birth? Who knows?

It was in 2010 that I began to identify with the parties of an investigation in a different manner. I now knew that I was meeting each person, survivor, witness and the accused for a purpose, or at least for a reason. I had been a part of co-creating each interaction, situation and circumstance with everyone. It was up to me to use it to the best of my ability for growth, empowerment and momentum towards my goals. My relationship to them, however brief, good or not so good, was directly related to what my journey as an adoptee had meant all along.

I began to interact with everyone as if they held a piece to my puzzle: A piece to more of my peace. As I began to respond to people differently, I gave and received information that helped us both and astounded us all. The cases themselves opened my mind to the metaphors of life all around me. Miracles were everywhere and had always been there whether I saw them or not. I learned that more people are affected by the separation from their original family than once believed by the masses and it affects people in a variety of ways. I realized that I was as much a part of their situations relative to surrender, relinquishment, abandonment, foster care, adoption and reunion with regard to biological families as they were to mine. I began to see profound connections with those not directly affected by adoption and how their family situations mirrored my experiences.

My understanding about relationships between people became clear that adoption was just one way families are formed and come together. Adoption can actually bring more people together who otherwise wouldn't cross paths. I consider it a good thing when people can be more connected and less separated from each other. I began to see adoption as a bridge instead of a wall. And while bridges are more difficult to build, they are designed to bring people together, reach new territories, and overcome obstacles. There are so many other ways people become relatives or come to know one another as family. However, the fact still remained that I had an original family that I wanted to see and I hoped wanted to meet me.

As my twenty-fourth year on the police department rapidly approached, seven outstanding officers who I had the privilege of working closely with during our careers had made their transitions. Det. Alfreda R. Rushing in 2005; Det. Harold D. Smalls on April 27, 2006; Det. Richard E. Peck, Sr. in May 2008; Det. Joseph M. Airhart, Jr. on November 4, 2008; Det. Thomas F. Ayers on August 14, 2009; Det. Maverick Porter on September 3, 2009; and Det. Elroy E. Baker on December 26, 2009. I attended each funeral service, mourned the earthly loss and was reminded of the gift of life. Though I said a silent prayer that they rest in peace, I knew that a piece of each of them I would carry with me throughout my life. Also, I gained more clarity about each death experience teaching us something in this life when we're willing to listen.

[9] Abraham-Hicks: Buffallo, NY September 25, 2001

[10] FamilyTreeDNA.com

Interlude – The Death Experience

LITTLE GIRL ON A PLANE

An atheist was seated next to a little girl on an airplane and he turned to her and said, "Do you want to talk? Flights go quicker if you strike up a conversation with your fellow passenger."

The little girl, who had just started to read her book, replied to the total stranger, "What would you want to talk about?"

"Oh, I don't know," said the atheist. "How about why there is no God, or no Heaven or Hell, or no life after death?" as he smiled smugly.

"OK," she said. "Those could be interesting topics, but let me ask you a question first. A horse, a cow, and a deer all eat the same stuff – grass. Yet a deer excretes little pellets, while a cow turns out a flat patty, but a horse produces clumps. Why do you suppose that is?"

The atheist, visibly surprised by the little girl's intelligence, thinks about it and says, "Hmmm, I have no idea."

To which the little girl replies, "Do you really feel qualified to discuss why there is no God, or no Heaven or Hell, or no life after death, when you don't know shit?"

And then she went back to reading her book.

You may have guessed that I see myself as the little girl in the humor of that joke. Sure, we learn a few things and gain an understanding in some areas, but there is still so much we don't know that we don't know about every subject. Nevertheless, we continue to engage in conversations with each other about a variety of topics to continue our growth. I have come to recognize that the loss, separation and grief associated with adoption has some parallels with my perception of death.

There are four major topics that are a part of a discussion at any given time among people: Sex, money, religion and DEATH. I would become quite acquainted with the real meaning of separation, loss and death before my son's first birthday. I had gone to many funerals. My grandparents', cousins', a host of friends and acquaintances were among the services I had attended over the years, but nothing came close to my dad's passing on February 28, 1991.

With every person's transition, I learn something that strengthens my faith. I learned from my dad's passing that relationships with people mean everything and that we must honor them. Value your family and friends with your time. That was my dad's mantra, and he lived it every day. He would pop in on me in the morning and wonder why breakfast wasn't ready for him, though I didn't know he was coming over to my house. He would drop in on anyone as if they were expecting him. It was fascinating to me how everyone always welcomed him, because they knew he didn't have to give them his attention or the time of day. He didn't have to make himself available to them. They appreciated that he thought enough to visit long and often.

In exploring the parallel between my police investigations and my personal life, there is no escaping the fact of death. It's the one thing that levels the playing field among all people. We all will leave our physical bodies behind at some point. The experience is thought by some – if not most – people to be a place of finality, heaven or hell. Loss and separation when compared to death is believed to be equally tragic: A hell on earth. Each case represents a series of events that change peoples' lives and can create a sense of despair for its survivors.

The purpose of each investigation allowed me to get more in touch with my feelings based on what happened, was happening, and was likely to happen in the future. As the police, I was a part of so many lives affected by the death of a loved one, and it built my emotional muscles. I repeatedly observed people and families try to design a new normal and put the Humpty Dumpty of their lives back together again. Some people were better at it than others, but I watched them all do it. A witness on a case painted a good picture for me once by saying, "I got myself together in order to come here and meet with you for this interview, but when I return home, I'm going to fall apart; to pieces all over again."

I put on my mental hard drive how most people were dealing with putting one foot in front of the other to continue moving forward in spite of the uncertainty of life. I reminded myself that I would seek to always engage in the truth of what makes us human and willing to be courageous enough to move beyond my own comfort zones too.

Early in my career as a patrol officer, I was assigned to assist in a traffic accident that involved a young man who had been hit by a car. Upon reaching the scene, I witnessed an emotionally distraught man kneeling down over the deceased victim. As we tried to disperse the gathering crowd, it was a somewhat chaotic event. It was the man's twin brother who had been struck and killed by a driver. It was a moment when I wondered about so many things at once. This man witnessed the tragic death – all in an instant - of a person, a family member, a brother, and someone who he shared months with in their mother's womb.

Whether it's an accident, homicide, suicide, SIDS or the 90-year-old whose heart just stops beating as she walks outside to empty the garbage, we in law enforcement come face to face with death on a regular basis. I learned to focus on the Chicago survivors and all the other aftermath. In later years and towards the end of my career, I started giving my attention to the question: What do we stand to learn from this present circumstance, and how do we plan to grow and be empowered by the situation?

When I met my fourth and final partner as a detective before my retirement, I had no way of knowing how powerful and meaningful that connection would be on my journey. We started our daily police tours together sometime in 2007. During a conversation likely in a squad car, I learned that both of our parents had already made their earthly transitions. Her dad in 1990, mine in 1991. My mom in 2002, and hers in 2003. We discussed where their remains were buried in Oakwood Cemetery, Chicago. The cemetery covers at least 183 acres. My dad is in Garden of Meditation Section X lot 284, grave b3, and my mom is in the same section, Lot 45, grave d4. Johnnie and I decided to have lunch there during one afternoon between work assignments and check on the gravesites of our parents. It was a very peaceful day.

I headed toward the location of my mother's headstone, because it was easiest to find and near a paved road. I had been unable to get plots for my parents closer to each other. Johnnie followed me and said, "Both my parents are in this same area of the Garden of Meditation." In disbelief, I responded, "Really?" Johnnie went on to say that she wasn't certain of the exact location, but she remembered them being buried in an area by that name. I located my mother's headstone and we paused there for a moment before proceeding a short distance to my father's headstone. While walking through the cemetery, Johnnie spotted her mother and father's headstone somewhere between my parent's burial sites. We paused and continued walking together as we took in this entire experience. We exchanged conversation about the chances of our fathers making their transitions around the same time and then our mothers too. The unbelievable likelihood of all four of them being buried in the same gigantic cemetery and in the same small area together was truly uncanny.

My father's light gray stone has praying hands on the upper left side. It was starting to look weathered by the years. It was on that day that I most remember believing that death is not the end, but rather a season or an opportunity for those who remain to gain more peace. I left the cemetery filled with a calm belief that all was very well with them and us.

7   A SEARCH FOR MY PERSONAL TRUTH

I was finally ready emotionally, and especially spiritually to trust the unknown.

As a police officer, you are a preliminary investigator, but it's usually not until you become a detective that the cases are personal or closer to you. As a detective, you are responsible for every single detail and are called upon in court to explain the full course of your investigation, sometimes years later. Every "i" dotted and "t" crossed is an understatement, because when a defense attorney gets ahold of your reports and looks you directly in the eyes, they are looking for errors made by you in order to win their case. Through the years, I became better equipped to know what skills I needed to successfully complete a task in arriving at the truth. Along with developing physical abilities of endurance with a career in policing, emotional muscles are needed the most to do such a job day in and day out. After working on so many sensitive cases, I was emotionally ready to face my personal truth. I hadn't seen or heard it all, but surely had experienced enough on the emotional scale to withstand whatever my outcome and history presented to me. I was finally ready, emotionally, and especially spiritually, to trust the unknown.

My son Andre, when prompted to share his feelings about my search for birth family members around his twentieth birthday, wrote the following:

"I think it's really cool that my mother is finally finding a little closure on the adoption issue. It is a lot more important than I originally thought it was prior to her inquiry. I'm also happy that I get to see step by step as she gets closer to her goal. I have learned from this experience so far and am very eager to learn more. I am very proud and happy for my mother. I wish her all the success when the adoption law is lifted and adoptees can finally view their birth certificates firsthand."

Over the years, my son and I had had conversations about his thoughts about my adoption that led me to believe that he really didn't see things through my lenses, but his own. He would share things like, "I forget that you were adopted. I don't understand how someone can just give up a child. I could never do that. Why would you care about them when they didn't care about you?" He simply didn't understand my concern about searching for our other family. In 2010, he eventually said, "If it's important to you, then it's important to me." I deeply appreciated that as I started the process of a search for our first family.

Some family and mostly friends repeatedly encouraged me to take the time and connect with chapter one of my life. The idea that there were possibly siblings and a host of other relatives out in the world that I didn't know troubled some people more than others. I, on the other hand, was happy with my life. Then one day, it occurred to me that I had a responsibility to my son and future generations. What we do now affects them just like past generations have affected us. The only biological person connected to me had a right to know all of his family, so this was not just about me. The possibility that other aunts, uncles, cousins and especially grandparents were his family too! I knew that if I could provide my biological child with answers, then I must get started on a search. Once my son told me, "If I learned that I was adopted, I would immediately want to find my birth mother," I knew it was time and that I had all the necessary blessings.

I kept a journal relative to initiating a search for my birth family and keeping notes came natural to me after two decades of report writing for the police department. I knew that relying on my memory would not be sufficient for something as important as processing all the information during my search.

-On April 27th, I submitted the application online with *The Locator*. It was the first time I heard, "We find more peace when we find all the pieces" by the show's star Troy Dunn (investigator, detective and therapist). The show was in its fourth season on WE-TV. My intentions were to give them virtually no information and expect them to find my birth family. They might have said, "Good luck with that!" A producer contacted me over a year later when I had forgotten all about the show, because my focus was on obtaining birth records on my own. I wanted to see in private my court adoption and adoption agency files that contained the information about what really happened in and around 1964. My entries continued on and on in my journal with each passing month in preparation. Before an actual meeting of my birth family, I believed that there were still necessary steps of finding out more information about the adoption community. I wanted to be as prepared as possible for the likely outcome of my reunion.

The day before my 46th birthday, I made a date to go to an open house at The Cradle House, 2049 Ridge Ave., Evanston, IL on May 2nd. I had heard a few things about this place and not all of it was good from mostly birth mothers and adult adoptee groups. They were not entirely comfortable with some of the practices of adoption agencies in general. The Cradle has been in existence since 1923 and I wanted to see for myself.

I met staff, adoptive parents, birth parents and Gale Sayers of The Sayers Center/The Cradle. It was the 33rd annual Open House on a Sunday when I set foot on the grounds. The agency's stately building sits on the southeast corner of a peaceful community in a northern suburb of Chicago. The sun shined brightly on the decorated entrance. It was a wonderful experience meeting Gale Sayers, his wife and many families brought together through The Cradle. The Director of Resource and Community Development was my host. He gladly explained the rich history of their adoption resources. Julie Tyler was the president at the time of the event.

It was such a good time for prospective adoptive parents (PAPs) and children too. Some of the activities at the open house included a petting zoo, face painting, tricks, balloons, temporary tattoos, cookie decorating, meeting local firefighters, and of course photographs taken with the legendary NFL Hall of Famer Gale Sayers. Refreshments in the dining room were tasty and were available for the entire three hours. This event was so well attended and an unforgettable time viewing three babies just days old in the nursery on the third floor waiting to be placed into adoptive homes.

While I enjoyed visiting The Cradle that day, it didn't compare to all the other information that was at my disposal and had been there all the time. I was smack dab in the middle of the National Foster Home/Care Month of May and I had never heard of it before then. The more I spoke with people about foster care and adoption, the more people I realized were directly or indirectly affected by separation from birth family members. I spent more and more time in the public library checking out books about people who were adoptees, birth and adoptive parents. I rented or purchased DVDs about adoption like "Secrets & Lies, "Antwone Fisher", "The Blind Side" and "Closer Than You Think", a documentary by Kyle Harris.

In Illinois, during November 2010, I took to the Internet to connect with agencies and organizations pertaining to the adoption community. The Internet engaged me for hours nearly everyday and I learned of The Midwest Adoption Center (MAC) and the Illinois Adoption Registry. I learned what adoption records were available in Illinois. MAC told me that the new Illinois adoption law would allow for the identity of my birth mother to be known and used in the search for a reunion provided a request had not been made to remove name(s). In the meantime, I could obtain my adoption decree from the Cook County Clerk of Illinois as advised by the Illinois Adoption Registry. It was possible to learn the exact date of my adoption in court, and the agency used in facilitating the case. By state law, I could obtain information from the adoption agency surrounding my surrender and adoption, but there would be no disclosure of the identity of biological family members. I would only receive non-identifying background information. I opted to complete any and all applications that could provide more answers.

I learned from MAC that Governor Patrick Quinn signed into law on May 29, 2010 the release of the original birth certificate to adoptees born after 1946 effective November 15, 2011. The Illinois Adoption Registry provided me with information to obtain my adoption decree and that document would prove to be my strongest lead in creating the possibility of a birth family reunion separate from obtaining my OBC.

The Internet has proven to be an excellent resource to the adoption community. Many people have been able to search and reunite with birth family members on Facebook and other social networks. Many websites have helped to create further communication between people for the sharing of names and photographs to stay connected in a meaningful way. I believe that with advancing technology, the adoption community will continue to expand in bringing families together.

Social media opened up a whole new world to me with groups on Facebook like Concerned United Birth parents (CUB), Bastard Nation, Adoptees Liberation Movement Association (ALMA), Family Life Services Adoption, Evan B. Donaldson Adoption Institute, Adoption Voices, The Gift of Adoption, and Chicago Area Families for Adoption. I asked anybody who would listen, "What do you think about adoption?" Most people responded, "I think it's okay. Why do you ask? Are you adopted?" "Yes. I am", I would respond. And then there were a few people who I had known for years at work, but only recently discovered our connection in the adoption community during general conversation.

One morning while at work, a supervisor noticed a book on my desk and asked me, "What's that you're reading?" "Oh, it's *"Twice Born: Memoirs of an Adopted Daughter"*, by Betty Jean Lifton. Until that moment he didn't know I was an adoptee, nor did I know that he and his wife have two sons under a closed adoption plan. I had known this person from work for over ten years and we had discussed many different things except this. I never knew until that day that we had the subject of adoption in common and were both members of that community. It confirmed two things for me: Adoption is not often discussed in even the closest of circles and more people than I thought are directly affected by it.

Towards the end of 2010, The White House issued a Presidential Proclamation declaring November as National Adoption Month. Meanwhile, I was being called to conquer this quest to know the truth, and I was closer to believing that a reunion with my birth family was only about one year away. I continued to stay tuned into Facebook and joined more groups. I was hearing the voices of the adoption community loud and clear in order to move me further along in my journey. One of the first adoptees that I met online was Melinda. She is the author of *A Legitimate Life* and writes about her birth family reunion. Melinda told me what makes her smile the most about being a part of the adoption community. She said, "Talking and reading what we all have to say about it." Melinda shed a light on what so many people are doing to facilitate change in the area of closed adoptions. She and I maintained contact via Facebook and by phone. I enjoyed engaging with other adoptees who were all wishing me the best.

8 BEING AN ADOPTEE IS A PART OF MY IDENTITY

As a detective, I was quite familiar with reports, procedures and abiding by the law.

It was January 24, 2011 while watching The Oprah Winfrey Show when I was happily reminded of the active search for my birth family that officially began in 2010.

Oprah introduced the world to her sister Patricia Lee, who was relinquished at birth on April 26, 1963. She first met Patricia during the Thanksgiving holiday season of 2010. In 2007, Patricia learned that she was related to Oprah, because they shared the same birth mother. Oprah was nine years old when Patricia was born and never knew at the time of a third sibling. Popular shows covered the news, and overnight Oprah was a part of the adoption community. While in the company of her mother and adopted sister Patricia, Oprah shared an epiphany that helps the adoption community move forward: "Let go of the shame."

On February 8, 2011, I applied by mail for my non-identifying background information from the Illinois Department of Public Health Vital Records, and on March 7, 2011 I received a letter in response about my birth mother that read as follows:

"The birth mother's age is listed as 17 (uncertain) at the time of your birth, the birth father's age is listed as 17 at the time of your birth and their races are both listed as negro. Your date and place of birth are May 3, 1964 at the Salvation Army Booth Memorial Hospital in Chicago, Illinois."

Again, on February 14th, I felt connected to the adoption community and knowing that I was moving forward in my search for the truth when the Oprah Winfrey Network aired a show "Searching for…" with Pam Slaton (a genealogist). The one thing that was apparent to me as an adoptee, was the relevance of being a part of the adoption community in one capacity or another sooner rather than later. Some of the shared stories were of closed adoptions. I could relate to their experience of not having access to information over decades.

It is a fascinating adventure and journey to discover that there is already a connection to others unknown to you at the present moment. Adoptees surrender to the laws that govern their state, the wishes of loved ones and personal ambivalence to search for answers. Most members of the closed adoption constellation (like no other group) are called upon to be patient throughout many, many years. When they choose a time to reconnect, they trust their instincts and hope for the best. Many of the outcomes bring the closure they envision to take them to the next level or not.

Pam Slaton's own story gave her closure and enabled her to fulfill her passion in life. She had 3000 solved cases and an 80% success rate in finding other people's birth family. After finding her own birth mother, she had been able to "learn and grow." While living in New Jersey, she invited people searching for family to her home and "wanted to be a best friend through the process." I wished I had more information, because maybe she could help me too. Though I was never moved to write her, I enjoyed hearing all the different adoption stories. One of my favorite episodes was learning that an adoptee had waited over forty years to learn that she has two biological brothers whom with she shares the same birth parents. I wondered if I had full siblings, too.

Investigative skills came naturally to me after twenty-four years in law enforcement. It was ironic that after two decades of searching for answers where the truth is paramount in criminal investigations, I met resistance. Every adoption related agency abided by the letter of the law. People made it clear that they were unable to share with me truthful information contained on documents that they were able to view about me. I was appreciative to be able to utilize my experience of interviewing people to obtain information, but all my skills certainly did not pay off during this time.

In March 2011, I mailed the request for my adoption decree. This document would hopefully contain another important piece of information so far. I would then have two strong leads in my case; the adoption agency who handled my placement and the hospital of my birth. I contacted the Salvation Army and John Larsen returned my call on March 10, 2011.

A face-to-face meeting with a representative from the Salvation Army had been granted to me on the same day that the event promoting adoption reform was taking place in New York City. Darryl McDaniels of DMC rap group was at the Hard Rock Cafe Times Square. *"Learning the Right Lessons About Adoption: What the Oprah Winfrey Reunion Teaches Us"* was spear-headed by Zara Phillips, McDaniels and Adam Pertman of the Evan B Donaldson Institute. Zara and Darryl performed their song, "I'm Legit" on stage followed by a panel discussion about the issue of adoptees and having the Right to access their original birth certificates. A tear-jerking video shown at the event featured individuals seeing their original birth certificates thirty, forty and even more years after birth, because their states had lifted the seal of their birth records. An organization called The Unsealed Initiative is one of many groups that challenge the laws relative to sealed records.

On March 11, 2011, I went to the place of my birth on the north side of Chicago at 5040 North Pulaski Ave. The large brick building on the west side of the street is currently The Salvation Army Metropolitan Divisional Headquarters. In 1964, it housed The Salvation Army Booth Memorial Hospital. I was greeted by John Larsen and shown photos of the facility when it housed a maternity ward on two floors. I viewed old photos of a bedroom at one time shared by two pregnant girls, a cafeteria, a classroom, an outdoor lounging area, a delivery room, a nursery and a chapel. Mr. Larsen spoke with me at length about the climate of the 1960s that sparked a need in the community for The Salvation Army to address unwed and unwanted pregnancy. He has been working at this headquarters since 2004.

According to Larsen, the pregnant girls and women weren't prisoners at the Salvation Army during their stay and were free to leave the facility. However, the vast majority did not return home until after giving birth. The girls were allowed to have visitors during their time there, but the girls' parents were most likely their more frequent guests. According to the Salvation Army, their facility during the entire time of the early to mid 20th century was considered one of the cleanest, safest and most comfortable places for a young pregnant girl. In fact, the hospital serviced women who were not staying in the section of the maternity home. The average age of a girl living in the home was fourteen years old, and there were all sorts of reasons why families heavily relied on the social services provided by the Salvation Army. In 1985, it closed its doors as a hospital due to the decline in providing the services of a maternity home. The Salvation Army continues to meet the needs of its community in a variety of different ways.

Mr. Larsen gave me a tour of the remodeled building that is now home to dozens of offices and Salvation Army personnel. I met current employees in offices that were once the nursery, the labor/delivery room or a birth mother's bedroom during her stay at the maternity home decades ago. Mr. Larsen pointed out original furnishings, fixtures and walls only changed by fresh paint. One of the only differences made to the chapel was the use of chairs instead of stationary seating to accommodate larger groups. Otherwise, the space used for worship, prayer and meditation by girls and women surrendering their babies back in the 1960s looks the same.

Before leaving Mr. Larsen, he heartwarmingly shared with me his experience as an adoptive parent. He told me how he and his wife had four children and the youngest were bi-racial males adopted at birth. In fact, his youngest son was born at the Salvation Army

Booth Memorial Hospital during its last couple years of existence. Mr. Larsen went on to tell me that when his boys were younger, he thought that they would be the closest as adoptees, but it turns out that his oldest son and oldest biological daughter are closer and the youngest son and his youngest biological daughter are more alike. I had many smiles and laughter with Mr. Larsen about the beauty of the adoption community. We agreed that it has truly touched so many lives for the better and will continue to do so into the future.

On March 15, 2011, I set my sights on traveling to Orlando, Florida for the annual AAC conference. The annual AAC event on April 13-17th 2011 would include keynote speakers and a host of workshops. I was particularly interested in Questions You Want Answered And Are Afraid to Ask, Searching For Family, Searching For Her and Finding Them: Connecting With Siblings, Long Term Reunion, and How To Write Your Adoption Story. I booked my flight and a room for two nights at the Florida Hotel and Convention Center with much anticipation and excitement.

I joined the AAC for $50, and spoke with representatives to get a roommate for the event. I corresponded and spiritually connected with Sherry Chait and learned that she was a birth mother who had surrendered a son over fifty years before. Sherry had reunited with her son (Marc) twenty-five years prior and he too was going to be at the AAC conference. I was excited about meeting both Sherry and Marc as a part of my journey.

Sherry Chait is a native of New York and became pregnant by her boyfriend when she was seventeen years old. Sherry's doctor convinced her that giving the baby up for adoption was in the best interests of her and the child. She now knows that the doctor was wrong. Sherry went on to marry another man and give birth to four other children, but always wanted to reunite with her first born. When the time and opportunity surfaced for Sherry to travel and meet Marc in Chicago, she went. She happily and tearfully recalled the plane ride:

"On the TWA plane, I was crying. A stewardess came over and asked why I was crying. I said I was going to meet my son for the first time since I gave him up for adoption. The stewardess sat with me and told me that she understood, because she gave up a child to adoption and the only person that knew was the man she married. Her parents never knew. She was very interested in hearing my story. Another passenger complained to the head stewardess that I was getting too much attention, so my story was explained to her. The stewardess had to explain to her supervisor that she too had given up her first born. When the plane landed, the crew held everyone back for me to exit first. The crew gave me a bottle of wine and said congratulations. Marc was there to greet me with flowers and a big hug. I believe with adoption that it is better to know than to not know."

On March 21, 2011, I received my adoption decree and learned that the Chicago Child Care Society (CCCS) handled my adoption in 1966. Now, one of the three documents I found among my mother's things when she died made sense. I placed a phone call and learned that the organization and building were still in the same Hyde Park community location as decades ago. I immediately contacted their office, but received no response. I contacted CCCS again on April 4, 2011 and spoke to Sandra Arrington who directed me to Curt Holderfield (director of child welfare post-adoption information). I wanted to see my file and learn about my start in life, but I understood the law. The process of gaining non-identifying background information is very straightforward. In the state of Illinois with a closed adoption, it simply means that an adoptee cannot be given names or addresses of the birth parent/s, birth family members or the adoptee's name at birth.

Mr. Holderfield told me that for $100.00, a letter from the Illinois Department of Public Health indicating that I had been placed in the Illinois Adoption Registry/Medical Information Exchange (IARMIE) program database, and a copy of my photo identification card, I could receive non-identifying information from my file in the form of a report. As a detective, I was quite familiar with reports, procedures and abiding by the law. I complied with all the requirements and waited to hear back from CCCS.

Meanwhile, the AAC's annual event couldn't come fast enough. I longed to spend a weekend of healing with members of the adoption community. Being an adoptee is a part of my identity, much like being female and black. I can't imagine being unable to gather together throughout my life with other women or other blacks, so it only makes sense that I would desire to connect with my adoption community.

Once settled in Orlando for the conference, I selected different workshops than initially planned based upon being a member of the closed 1960's adoption era like Searching for Family, Searching for Her and Finding Them, and Bookends: Annette Baran & BJ Lifton-"The Pioneers of Adoption Reform" with Jean A.S. Strauss. I formed instant bonds with several members of the constellation. One of the most powerful parts of the conference were keynote speakers Deann Liem, "In The Matter of Cha Jung Lee" and Dr. Ron Nydam, "What's the Good in Adoptive Development".

"Children of adoption may grow up well, but they do grow up differently" is a quote from Dr. Ron Nydam's book *Adoptees Come of Age*. Dr. Nydam explores the adoptee's relinquishment and adoption experience as a continual life-long process of two separate life events. His book acquaints the adoption community and others with honoring the adoptees' two very different lived experiences. Dr. Nydam is good at acknowledging for the adoptee a clear distinction between relinquishment and adoption, which has been often disregarded by society. A quote in the book's introduction from Elizabeth Starr – "I hate my relinquishment. I love my adoption" – best defines how some adoptees do experience two profoundly different, yet joint events in their life. Relinquishment means to give up something to another person. Adoption means to give official acceptance or approval of someone.

While at the 2011 AAC conference, I listened to dozens of people from the constellation and learned individual accounts of their experience in the adoption community. Here are a handful of briefly shared stories from adoptees and birth parents from various parts of the country and Canada:

-A birth mom from Canada surrendered a baby girl at birth over forty years ago as a result of feeling pressured to comply with the wishes of others at the time ended in a tricky set of circumstances. When she found her daughter working as a nurse in a hospital, she stalled on identifying herself on the initial encounter for fear of rejection. She then chose a gradual reunion that proved successful and resulted in a good relationship with her biological daughter built overtime.

-Krista McCoy Woods was adopted at three months in 1973 from a foster home. She is bi-racial and was raised on the south side of Chicago by white parents. She had not seen her original birth certificate when we met, but was able to reunite with her biological father in 1995. On April 29, 2011, Krista announced her new position as Illinois State Representative for the AAC. It was during the AAC conference when she and I met and realized that we lived in the same state of Illinois and frequented the same neighborhoods. We hadn't been able to connect until going to Florida. The AAC made it possible for our connection through a gathering of the adoption community. We also learned that we were both at the CAFFA event earlier in the year.

During an interview with me, Krista responded to the question "What is the most important thing about being a member of the adoption community?" She said, "Knowing that I have people who can understand and relate to me – my challenges, hopes, dreams – at any given time...knowing that I am a part of the triad and empowered...there is solidarity in our numbers...it (the issue of adoption) transcends age, race, gender, culture, and ethnicity."

-Charlene from Florida was pregnant in 1989 when she utilized an attorney to find adoptive parents for her baby girl after a couple she had previously found backed out of the agreement on the day she gave birth to her. Charlene's decision to relinquish her baby over twenty years ago never changed her desire to be reunited with her adult daughter in the future. She utilized search angels to locate her daughter and believes "the most important thing is to never regret your decision and to never be alone with that decision. The community helps us with not feeling alone and to remind us that we did what we did for different reasons and to be ok with those decisions. Only until the 1980's have we been able to talk openly about adoption."

-Betty Lou from New Jersey unwillingly surrendered her baby boy after delivering him in the 1960's and always wanted to reunite with her son. With older closed adoption practices, she felt it wasn't her right to search for her son since he was placed with another family. His diligence in finding her prevailed over sealed records in their state and a reunion has truly been one of good new beginnings.

-Titia Ellis' book, *The Search* describes how she remembered a discussion of her adoption at the age of three, eight and eleven. She shares in her memoir about being adopted in the 1930s and living in a small town outside of Chicago. "Adoption was a taboo subject for Titia Ellis growing up. In mid-life she felt inspired to search for her birth mother. Along the way, she met unforeseen obstacles at every turn. But in the end, what she discovered transformed her life."

-In Minnesota, birth mother and daughter (Jackie Maher and Katie DeCosse) co-authored a book, *Fifty Years in 13 Days* after reuniting in 2007. Jackie states in the book, "I am a birth mother. Years (after the 1950s) became decades and somewhere along the way the rules changed. Some people have remarked on the length of time (my age!) that has passed; I think they assume that it is done earlier in life or not at all."

It was on a Friday morning of April 15, 2011 when I peeked through the door of a semi-dark room filled with about fifty people seated around tables with all eyes on a video masterfully created by author, filmmaker and adoptee, Jean A.S. Strauss. I immediately grabbed a seat in the back of the room as not to disturb the moment. Strauss was only about ten minutes into this particular workshop at the AAC conference. There was still enough time to learn from the film and various speakers about two pioneers in adoption reform who I would never meet in person. Each one (Annette Baran and Betty Jean "BJ" Lifton) had made their earthly transition in 2010. Meeting Jean Strauss that day would forever change my search for the better.

As of May 2011, for an adoptee born prior to 1946, the laws in Illinois were rather strict, but medical, education, employment, religion and the circumstances surrounding relinquishment followed by adoption were all considered non-identifying information that could be shared with an adoptee.

During the ride from Orlando back to Chicago, I was anxious to hear from Mr. Holderfield about my adoption file. A day after my forty-seventh birthday, I received a call from him. CCCS had completed the report summarizing my two-year background file with the agency. I went to Holderfield's office and retrieved part of the first chapter of my life. The letter was dated May 3, 2011. What a wonderful birthday gift. It had been exactly four weeks since my request for this information from CCCS when I learned the following:

"You were born on (Sunday) 5/3/64 at 1:18AM and weighing 6lbs. 15oz. and 20 inches long and in good physical condition. Labor was noted to be 13 hours 25 minutes. After delivery you were initially placed in a foster home with the Smith family."

Included in the manila envelope containing the CCCS report was a photo of me at six months old. Until that moment as I sat in my car with the sun shining brightly outside of the CCCS building, I had never seen a picture of myself prior to 1966. As a healthy baby in only a diaper, I was sitting on the lap of an unknown woman. I went on to read about other information taken from the adoption file:

"It is indicated in your file that your biological mother sought help in planning your adoption through the Family Services Bureau (FSB) who requested placement and possible adoption through Chicago Child Care Society (CCCS) upon your birth.

"According to your file, Family Service Bureau United Charities of Chicago (FCB) referred your biological mother for the placement of her baby (you), due 4/23/64. It is indicated in a FSB referral letter that your biological mother first contacted the Family Service Bureau on 2/26/64. She phoned for an appointment for help planning for her pregnancy, requesting adoption and maternity home placement. At the time she emphasized her interest in continuing school which she had attended until 2/25/64. The FSB social worker met with your biological mother four times, two of which your maternal grandmother participated in as well. It is indicated in this letter that although they met a number of times, the background information is limited due to your biological mother's emotional difficulty in communication."

I continued reading.

"This referral letter goes on to say that your biological father is a 17 year old boy whom your biological mother has known for two years. It is stated that your biological mother had been dating him behind her parents' back and they have no knowledge of his background. Nothing else about your biological father is stated in your file and neither the Family Service Bureau nor Chicago Child Care Society had any contact with your biological father, nor was any information provided by your biological mother."

I read the entire six page summary from CCCS at least three different times and took special notice of the following:

"Your biological mother is a light skinned girl with clear complexion. She has large attractive eyes, thin nose and very little chin. She is quite thin, 5' 7" tall and she normally weighs around 130 pounds. She has straight black hair. She describes the putative father as of medium brown complexion, under 6', heavyset, muscular build. He dropped out of high school at the age of 17. Your maternal grandmother is of medium brown complexion and resembles your biological mother except that her chin is more prominent. Your maternal grandfather is of medium height and has a light freckled complexion and brown curly hair. He has a round face.

"You are described as 'an alert, attractive child of medium coloring with huge dark eyes, soft curly hair which your foster mother braids and a pretty mouth. She is a large-sized baby of sturdy build and excellent muscle strength and coordination." I felt mixed emotions for members of my family still unknown to me at this time as I continued to read the most revealing information received from CCCS to date. Concerning the referral made by FSB is the following paragraph:

"…the FSB social worker phoned CCCS and stated, 'during the recent interview with your biological mother, she (FSB social worker) had learned that there was considerable mental illness in the family. Two of your maternal grandmother's sisters had been quite disturbed, emotionally, possibly paranoia, and one had attempted to kill someone. The maternal grandfather had suffered a 'nervous breakdown,' although this might have been due to old age…this past year your maternal grandfather started to run out in the street, partially clothed, making angry threats. This would appear to be senile psychosis. However he has received no professional treatment'."

(Dated June 16, 1964)

"Throughout our contact with your biological mother we have found her to be a very disturbed girl. We feel that her deep-seated anger is related to failure of her parents to meet many of her needs. They speak of her mood during which she will sit in the corner and suck her thumb, but they give no indication that they have tried to reach out to her in any way. It was only after we encouraged your biological mother to ask her parents, that they visited her at the hospital. Due to the evident anger behind her withdrawal we do not feel that there is any evidence of schizophrenia. Due to your biological mother's withdrawal it is difficult to access her intellectual capacity…it is evident that her emotional problems are long standing, they may well interfere with school achievement."

"As of this date, your biological mother is very ambivalent about placement of the baby. It is our impression that, in some way, she recognizes that she is unable to meet the demands of caring for a baby yet she is unwilling to give up any part of herself. She wants to see the baby and plans are being made with the CCCS social worker for her to see the baby in the viewing room of your agency, without the presence of the foster mother. Both maternal grandparents give verbal recognition that your biological mother's own needs are so great that she cannot adequately care for a baby. However, their ambivalence is also apparent."

I learned that both of my birth parents were teenagers at the time of my birth. I had resided with the Smith family as a foster child for the first two years of my life before being permanently placed in July of 1966 with my adoptive parents. Was this true about mental illness? Was any of this true? Only time would tell. The CCCS report further stated:

"You appear to be a well adjusted 2 year old girl, bright and independent though not vivacious who needs an adoptive placement. She is receiving excellent care in the Smith family home since four days of age. Our goal is to support the excellent care given by the Smiths as long as you remain there and to help them release her (you) in adoption."

"The CCCS social worker agreed to place you in the adoptive home of the Ghostons. You were placed (July 1966) with the Ghostons on an adoptive basis... It goes on to say that 'the family consists of Mr. and Mrs. Ghoston and you who will be called Jennifer Dyan Ghoston.' It is noted that after placement 'you continued to be well with only occasional colds'...The adjustment during the supervision has been good. This appears to be a good placement."

"Jennifer who was three in May, was placed with Halscy and Clarice Ghoston, 50 and 42 years of age. We felt adoptive placement imperative for her rather than have her continue in foster care after it was found that the Smith family could not adopt her. You had excellent care in only one home and was above average in ability. The Ghostons are a mature couple who are ready for children and ready to make the adjustments and sacrifices necessary. They are warm people who can provide emotional security, value ability and will provide stimulation for you. We feel they can provide you with an excellent home with affection and stimulation in her formative years and that Mrs. Ghoston is young enough to continue care into your early adulthood. The adjustment during the supervision has been good. This appears to be a good placement."

"According to your file the adoption had been legally consummated on May 25, 1967 and your case was closed. CCCS

104

has had no further contact with your biological or adoptive parents."

By my son's twenty-first birthday, I had learned that there may not be enjoyment or enthusiasm as a result of the search, find and reunion. There may only be acceptance. I was okay with that. There is still peace in acceptance. I was learning to distinguish between the outcome and the search itself.

I considered just how many more adoption stories are out there and how many of them I would hear before meeting with members of my birth family. I wished I could hear them all, because no two adoptions are the same. Some adoptions were completely closed as in my case. Others were either semi-closed or open adoption plans. I believed if I could hear enough members of the constellation share their journey, the better I would feel about moving forward towards my reunion.

It seems unimaginable to start from a chapter one instead of chapter two and known my birth parents from the beginning many years ago. I perhaps had siblings that I could have had knowledge of and a relationship with over these forty plus years. There is also the thought of a relationship between other extended family members especially aunts, uncles and cousins. I was passionate about my son knowing his biological maternal side of the family, yet nearly impossible to really fathom after all this time.

I wrote Curt Holderfield at CCCS:

"I want to express my sincere appreciation for your assistance in helping me obtain more information concerning my adoption. I thank you for sending some medical information and a photograph from 1964. I was hoping you would consider reviewing my file. Please consider releasing more non-identifying background."

At times, I became increasingly frustrated with Mr. Holderfield's inability to provide me with information based on state law. He could see things written about my first two years that would never be as important to him as it was to me. He too felt a sense of frustration.

In June, he responded in a four-page letter, saying, "I have taken some time to go back through your file. Your biological mother wanted to conceal her pregnancy from neighbors and her two younger brothers, age 15 and 12…"

I considered just how important more rather than less information is in helping to establish a possible reunion or meeting with my birth family. I wondered were my interviewing skills serving me or was Mr. Holderfield being touched in a positive way by the issue of adoption by sharing more information from my file. I now knew of two uncles who were possibly still alive and well. If they had children, then there are likely first cousins to meet too. All of these small pieces made me enthusiastic and very interested in future possibilities.

In the meantime, I continued to immerse myself in adoption related issues from all angles to gain a clear understanding of the entire adoption community. That's what I believed good detectives did: gather as much information as possible before drawing conclusions and moving forward.

On July 5, 2011, one of the most interesting stories covered by Leah Hope, a Chicago reporter for ABC aired on the evening news about a new law in Illinois. A birth mother represented by attorney Linda Coon is noted as the first person in the U.S. to adopt four of her children upon the death of the adoptive parent. Yolanda Miller was given a second chance at legally being a mother to her children, after her mother (the adoptive parent) died in 2005. Also featured in this story was Illinois State Representative Sara Feigenholtz who stated, " Laws should fit people and their real lives". DCFS estimates 500 children are orphaned each year when an adoptive parent dies. The new law currently pertains to those adoptions by biological family members. This would be the first time I heard anything about State Rep. Feigenholtz and exactly what role she was playing relative to adoption reform in the state of Illinois. It wouldn't be long before I recognized the impact of this woman on the adoption community as an adoptee herself.

I noticed that adoption reform was championing slowly, but surely when on July 1, 2011, the governor of Rhode Island signed legislation allowing adoptees there the right to get their OBC at 25 years of age. Sen. Rhoda E. Perry and Rep. John M. Carnevale sponsored the legislation.

On July 29, 2011, I learned my home during my first two years was with the Smiths at 6942 S. Normal Ave., 2nd, 60621, a two-story brick building. The ages of the children in the home upon my arrival were nine, eleven, thirteen, fifteen and seventeen.

On August 19, 2011, I went to an address in Justice, Illinois with a picture of me on the lap of an unknown woman. I suspected that it was a woman named Willia Smith holding me and I was somewhat certain that I had located one of her sons Danny Smith, who was eleven years old in 1964. I entered the multi-unit building and went to the fourth floor. As I walked the hallway, I observed a man fitting the description of the man I was looking for. He was emptying the garbage. I called out, "Danny" and he turned around to see me. He stopped in his tracks as I approached him while holding the photo of me at six months old.

I talked swiftly as I explained that I was a foster child in 1964 in his parents' home. I held up the photograph that I wanted him to look at of me and told him that I believed the woman in the picture to be his mother. He held the photo and looked at me and back at the picture. He recognized his mother immediately and said, "Yes, that's my mother." He invited me inside of his apartment while still looking at the photograph. He introduced me to his girlfriend as I sat down at the kitchen table. He was in total amazement about my appearance at his doorstep that morning. He hadn't remembered me, but stared at his mom in the photo and knew it was her. He looked so much like his mother and his girlfriend said he looked more like Mrs. Smith than any of her other children.

Danny called his brothers, Ronald and James Jr., but not before I answered several questions. I volunteered as much information as possible, like the Normal Avenue address, the ages of his siblings and his mother's birth date. I gave him all the information known to me from my file. His youngest brother Ronald knew me as

Bonnie and said his mother would always put bonnets on me. He was often around his mother, being the youngest of his siblings, and had been the one to spend the most time with me. He recalled how he helped care for me on many occasions. The oldest brother, James Jr., remembered me too. He had consoled his mother about not being able to keep me after the finalization of my adoption.

Danny talked with me for two hours about his family and his mother in particular. Both of his parents had passed years before and he promised to locate their obituaries. A brother, Maurice, had passed of cancer at the age of twenty-four, and his only sister wouldn't be available to speak with me until a later time. I had decided to find the Smith family once I learned from CCCS's file about my two years with them. In my journal dated August 22, 2011, I wrote: "Danny and his girlfriend asked me why I hadn't searched (for my birth family) before now. I just answered, 'Because, God's timing is now and not then.' They were glad about my visit and assured me that they would do everything within their power to help me locate my birth family. I am excited about my journey as it continues to unfold with each miracle."

Meeting Danny was the most emotional experience so far. Through him, I felt his mother's love and the person responsible for starting the process of me feeling loved in a nurturing home. Danny seemed like such a caring, compassionate and spiritually connected person. I felt relieved to know that my first two years had been spent with his family. I could only imagine how well his mother must have cared for me on the fourth day of my life until 1966.

On November 14, 2011, I met Illinois State Representative Sara Feigenholtz and Melisha Mitchell, a birth mother already in reunion with her daughter adopted over thirty years ago. They were instrumental in changing the law in Illinois to allow adoptees the right to see their original birth certificate. It was good to finally meet these two persistent and tenacious women in the adoption community. Mitchell stated to the press, "Illinois adoptees are now 1st class citizens. 250,000 adoptees here get to request their OBC."

On the following morning at 10:00am, I requested my OBC in

person by driving from Chicago to Springfield and standing in line with other adoptees at the Illinois Department of Public Health Vital Records building. Fred, a good friend was great company during this opportunity to apply in person for my OBC. He had agreed to accompany me without question to the southern tip of Illinois for such an emotional occasion. It was a no brainer for Fred to share in what would be an unforgettable time.

It was my first time in the state's capital. The sun was shining brightly as Fred parked across the street from a small white brick structure with black letters and a green awning at 930am on November 15, 2011. He had been to this town before, but for nothing nearly symbolic as someone like me applying for their OBC. He was all smiles, because he knew of its importance seeing others waiting to apply too. I accepted an interview from a local reporter while I waited to be allowed inside of the office to apply for my OBC. I interviewed briefly with Jean Strauss about how it felt to finally be at this point in my life.

I was told that it would be four to six weeks from November 16, 2011 when I would see my OBC for the first time. A range of emotions would likely surface within me, because it has been an interesting journey of waiting to receive such important information. During one of my interviews with Jean Strauss on November 17, 2011, I shared the following in summary and not verbatim based on having no identifying information about my birth parents:

Q. What does not having my OBC mean to me?

A. Feelings of unworthiness, grief and powerlessness, then anger about others in government and the private sector being able to access a document that means more to me than it will ever mean to them. Disappointment and frustration turned to hopefulness with my adoption community. There was optimism because of the new Illinois law. Feelings turned again to positive expectations and enthusiasm about my search for birth family members. There is freedom in knowing the truth and releasing the shame and secrecy.

Q. How important is it to receive my OBC?

A. Besides the obvious benefit of medical information, the continuity of one's life is natural and normal. My journey didn't start at Chapter Two and Chapter One is equally important to my entire story. Adoptees under closed records do grow up and receiving our OBC is one of the most empowering events. It is a healing experience after going so many years without the benefit of being better connected to my beginnings. I laughingly expressed the feeling of completing the application to request my OBC. I filled out multiple request forms since learning of the new Illinois law, because of my excitement in having the right to finally make such a request. I understand that only one request form is needed, but I submitted two for $15.00 each, so I could see my OBC from the State of Illinois not once, but twice. I know it sounds strange.

It felt like my whole life had prepared me for the moment of December 13, 2011, 12:08pm as I sat across from my son and heard the voice on the other end of my phone. My original birth certificate had arrived to State Rep. Sara Feigenholtz's north side Chicago office through the U.S. Postal Service. I had been previously asked by State Rep. Feigenholtz and filmmaker Jean Strauss to consider opening my OBC on camera with other adoptees for the whole country to observe the significance of this access. On January 1, 2012, I decided on a date of January 15, 2012 for a celebration with the entire adoption community.

I had planned to open my OBC at that time in front of witnesses and agreed to have it mailed to State Rep. Feigenholtz. Jean Strauss wouldn't be in Chicago to authentically capture my reading it until January. I hadn't completely processed what that commitment really meant until the day I was sitting in a Friday's Restaurant in Oak Lawn, IL having a meal with my son Andre.

"It's entirely up to you. You can open it now or wait," said the voice on the phone. I replied, "No, I'll wait." Andre was the only one to truly appreciate my decision to wait an entire month before opening the envelope. He completely understood me when I said, "I've been waiting all these years, so I can wait a little longer." Family and friends didn't understand and repeatedly asked, "How can you not open it now?" I couldn't explain it to them any better than, "I'm used to waiting, but most importantly, I have come to an understanding that the adoption community deserves my full participation. I was totally committed to being a part of adoption reform by being open, honest and public. I told all listening ears that the new Illinois Adoption Law has changed, and it states:

"Illinois law now allows adopted adults born in Illinois prior to January 1, 1946, to obtain a copy of their original birth certificate listing the names(s) of their birth parent(s) by filing a Request for Non-Certified Copy of an Original Birth Certificate for with the Illinois Adoption Registry and Medical Information Exchange (IARMIE), which is administered by the Illinois Department of Public Health. Starting November 15, 2011, adopted adults born in Illinois after January 1, 1946, may obtain a copy of their original birth certificate listing the names(s) of their birth parents(s) by filing a Request for Non-Certified Copy of an Original Birth Certificate for with IARMIE." [11]

One particularly important paragraph out of four stated:

"Birth parents of adopted persons born in Illinois after January 1, 1946, may request that their name be removed from all copies of an adopted adult's original birth certificate release during the birth parent's lifetime by filing a Birth parent Preference form with IARMIE after January 1, 2011. To ensure anonymity, the Birth Parent Preference form should be filed prior to November 15, 2011." I truly hoped that it wasn't the case that my birth mother would want to remain anonymous to me.

I went on to use my career in law enforcement as an example of why my OBC is the next logical step. A search for the truth and finding it during a criminal investigation can turn good decisions into better ones. Many lives are affected best by having more rather than less information pertaining to the facts involving any given incident. In the case of closed adoptions and sealed records, the sharing of medical truths are far reaching possibilities in great decision making.

I considered what new legislation in Illinois and elsewhere helps adoptees further relate to their beginning chapter of life. I delighted in having access to all records currently maintained by adoption agencies, hospitals and city/state/county offices. I desired to have the right to see my entire file with CCCS that contained much more information than found on an OBC. Perhaps in the near future I would sponsor a "Bonnie bill" to change the law for the purpose of seeing all of the information currently held by a variety of institutions involved in the adoption process. Time will tell if even more truths can be obtained in this lifetime. Pumping my brakes was in order, because I was moving too far ahead of myself. By New Year's Day of 2012, I still didn't have my hands on my OBC yet, nor information about my birth family.

[11]www.idph.state.il.us/vitalrecords/vital/non_certified.htm

9 THE WAIT IS OVER

For me, seeing my original birth certificate gives me information that will confirm what I've been told all these years.

The moments prior to the event on Sunday, January 15th (Dr. King's birthday), I was excited beyond belief. I invited family, friends, lawmakers and adoption community members. Nearly everyone shared in my enthusiasm about this upcoming occasion for days, but perhaps my son's anticipation was the sweetest of all. He would now have access to information on my OBC as important to me as to him. I hoped that I would not emotionally explode during the gathering, so I remembered to breathe. I wanted to completely take in the experience of finally knowing more of the truth.

The band loaded equipment into the Ida Noyes Hall at the University of Chicago for live music and were to be a pleasant surprise for everyone. The orange balloons and linen tablecloths decorated the room. Jean Strauss, the filmmaker had set up her cameras to capture two different angles and was ready to videotape me opening my OBC. Surprisingly, I wasn't too nervous as about 60 people filled the room not really sure of what to expect with this celebration. I just believed that it was going to be a great time for everybody. Adoptees that I met for the first time that day were just as excited about this event, because we were all in this together. I had a speech prepared, but forgot to bring it. I went off the cuff something like this:

"Well, the time has finally come. Forty-seven years later, I get the right to request my birth certificate, receive it and today open it for the first time; an original birth certificate. For most of you, you've been with your original families and you've had your original birth certificate and you really haven't thought too much about it. You thought it was just an ordinary document. But, for adoptees here in Illinois, it's an extraordinary piece of paper to be able see for the first time."

"In about an hour probably less than that, I'll be opening my birth certificate and you'll be witnessing it. For me, seeing my original birth certificate gives me information that will confirm what I've been told all these years. Hopefully it will contain my birth mother's name. This is a very emotional time just to have the right. I kind of looked at being able to request the document, receive it and open it as three different phases. I've been satisfied and very relieved just to know that I have it now. I want to give you the short version of my adoption story."

Through a jittery voice and tears of joy that wanted to flow off and on at times, I continued speaking to those I love, and concluded my speech by saying:

"I've realized over these 21 years that you Andre are the only person that I know of being biologically related to." A collective, "Wow" could be heard across the room. "That's deeply meaningful to me and special. So, I thank you for being my son and being willing to take this journey with me." Andre responded, "Thank you for letting me take this journey with you."

I went on with a shaky voice;

"And so now, I want to introduce to you someone you've got to meet and hear from before you leave here today. She has been tireless and tenacious in her efforts against some of the toughest critics. They don't want to see us have our original birth certificates as adoptees. And so there's one word that comes close to describing how I feel, appreciative for your passion and persistence down state."

State Rep. Sara Feigenholtz obliged me by saying a few words to the group. "This is Jennifer's moment and I am going to speak and only talk about how amazing this journey has been for me, because of the people that I've met. I just hope that her brothers and sisters (of the adoption community) in every other state in this country could have these kinds of moments and could have these kinds of celebrations. I find it very, very appropriate that it's happening on Martin Luther King (birthday) weekend, because today I'm going to open my birth certificate. This morning also I wrote on my Facebook page, 'free at last' and I really mean it."

I invited other adoptees, family and friends to give some remarks. I started by saying, "Sometime last year, I made a commitment that I'd be honest and I'd be public in the hopes of dispelling the fears and the ignorance associated with adoption."

Danny Smith spoke first, "How you all doing today? Jennifer Ghoston. We don't know her by that name. To us her name is Bonnie. She was persistent in finding out who her real birth parents were. I'm just up here today just to say thank you for finding us. And the best thing I can say on behalf of the Smith family, we love you."

Ronald spoke next, "I talked to Bonnie, and I said, 'Bonnie I babysat you. On this trip coming up to see my brother, I was bringing him some pictures and I was looking through the chest and everything. There it is, I found it. And there is a lot of information in there and this is for you." My foster mother, Willia Mae Smith's obituary was given to me by Ronald as I was moved to tears. A total of ten people stood before the group and spoke which included Gail Tubbs who shared a most unexpected story for the group.

Gail shared, "I felt sad and my heart ached for adoptees who are searching for their birth parents. I needed to share what it felt like having to make a decision to give up your child, There were various reasons I ended up putting my child up for adoption. About ten years later, I decided to start looking for that child. That's when I learned that the records were sealed. They didn't want to give me any information. Somebody suggested that I hire an attorney. I tried several attorneys. Nobody would touch the case. Alright, that was in the 70s. Went past the 80s into the 90s and started looking for my son again. And I continued for several years using locator services that they were advertising on Oprah and all that stuff."

I was glad that Gail shared her story and once again respected her courage. She continued her story by saying, "I went on the internet keyed in the word adoption. A website called ReunionRegistry.com cropped up real quick. And so I put in all of my information and they said possible match. I'm like, you know these people need to stop. They shouldn't play with people's emotions like that. The very next day when I came home from work I had a voicemail on my phone and it said call Reunion Registry. We think there is a possible match or something like that. Come to find out, it was my son looking for me. He had been registered with that agency for about five years."

Fred said these words that I won't soon forget:

"I just want to say this, it's all about love and when we share love and respect there's nothing that won't happen. The miracles are happening as this miracle happened now; today's a brand new day. We're in the afternoon of a brand new day; one that we've never seen before; clean and unused. And it's up to each of us to give what we have to each other to continue on this journey called life. And at the end of it acknowledge that God is in control of it all. I want to thank you for allowing me to just say that to you. Thank you, Jennifer, for being my friend."

My son spoke:

"How's everybody doing today? Everybody's good. I would like to say, I'm appreciative and thankful to the Lord that I'm able to see my own birth certificate and I know my biological mother and I love you mom. I'm just real blessed to be here and thankful to be here. I really don't have much to say, but this is real important to my mom, so it makes it important to me. I just want to thank everyone for coming out, just glad to see everybody. I'm holding my mom's birth certificate which she'll see for the first time today which is very powerful."

After my request that the band play, K. Jon's "My Ship Has Finally Come", I read my OBC for the first time in front of everybody there. I was overwhelmed with emotion to see that I was born May 3, 1964 at 1:18 A.M. just like I had been told all these years. Finally viewing my original birth certificate confirmed it among other things. I had asked everyone in the room what did they first want to know listed on my OBC and the overwhelming answer was, "Your given name." I saw my name typed on a line, so I shared, "Bonnie Lynne Upshaw." Line 7 was blank. It was supposed to contain my birth father's name. Line 12 listed Wanda Nell Upshaw as my birth mother, and her signature was located on Line 17. This extraordinary piece of paper in the form of my OBC was filed on May 6, 1964 and was finally in my hands. It felt wonderful. The room was filled with everyone who took in this moment and I can't imagine reading from this document for the first time without them being there. I briefly thought back to some Upshaws I knew in high school and silently thanked God that I never dated any of them. It was an awesome time being caught on film by Jean Strauss for her film *A Simple Piece of Paper*, and I could not have had a better time during such a momentous occasion.

Everyone stayed for an extended time to dance, mingle and look at my OBC. The band fittingly played Maze Featuring Frankie Beverly, "Joy and Pain" and it was indeed how I felt to consider all these years being denied the right to hold my OBC. Oh, but what joy over pain to finally have it for the rest of my life. The most frequently asked question was, "Why didn't you read aloud your birth mother's name?" I told them "Maybe she would want anonymity." In the event that she wanted her privacy, I would respect that since the event was being filmed and going to be in the public eye. I wanted to respect her right to privacy.

On January 16, 2012, with the help of Melisha Mitchell, a searcher and advocate for adoption reform, I learned that my birth mother had passed on March 17, 1996, moments after her forty-ninth birthday. I was actually quite prepared for this news, because of all the research I had done in preparation for a reunion with my birth family. It is often the case that birth mothers have made their transition before a reunion between them and the child they relinquished at birth. I immediately accepted the news of Wanda's death and forged ahead to find other family members. I knew they were out there and I was hopeful that they were waiting to hear from me. The idea that I may have siblings, first cousins and a host of other relatives excited me as I continued my journey. I also believed that my life as an adoptee had been for purpose. It had provided me a very clear and present understanding of my life, especially if my birth family had been praying for my well-being. Every single thing about my life had prepared me for this point in time.

Of the many questions asked by family and friends by the time I was closing in on a reunion with the maternal side of my birth family, two things stood out the most to me: "Why did I wait so long to begin my search for my birth family? As a member of law enforcement in search of the truth, how were you able to hold your curiosity for over twenty-five years?"

These were great questions that were similar in nature. I answered them both, "As adoptees, we typically have a need to protect our adoptive parents. We never want them to think that we are not appreciative for having them as parents. Adoptive parents usually feel threatened by the idea of us reuniting with our birth parents. I knew my mother on three separate occasions expressed her dislike about me searching for my birth mom and I did not want her to experience pain about the subject. So much so that I placed her wishes above my own for nearly ten years after her death. I believe that the right time to search is when you're ready; no matter the reasons, and you don't have to make any apologies about it.

During my full year of research on adoption in preparation for my reunion, I also studied the Law of Attraction, which states that we attract into our life whatever we think about. Our dominant thoughts or vibrations will find a way to manifest. As stated by Abraham-Hicks, "We acknowledge many times you are born into an environment where well-being isn't flowing". I wondered if somehow it might be some truth to a wee little infant setting an intention through their energy and not there ability to speak to co-create a space and place in this life that was bigger than remaining with their original family; an extraordinary life that could be an example to the world of the bigness of family. It also made sense that my years in law enforcement had given me a certain amount of credibility in the eyes of those outside of the adoption community. I was creating the opportunity for adoption reform to be better understood by people who had always been with their birth families. I did that on what would have been Dr. King's eighty-third birthday.

One of my beliefs throughout the years of my childhood, puberty and as a young adult was being an adoptee is a lifelong process. The beauty has always been that with each reunion story, adoptee connection and hurdle over obstacles in adoption reform, we in the community all feel just a little more relief about our journey. By the time I opened my OBC as a result of Illinois adoption laws changing in the favor of open records, I was excited about other states like Ohio and New Jersey getting closer to changing their laws too.

10   IN REUNION

"We didn't know how to find you, but she always said that you would come here."

-Juanita Upshaw

I've known for many years that I would likely one day write a book. I didn't know when or exactly what it would be about until I read three quotes by Maya Angelou. She spoke to me: "If you get, give. If you learn, teach." "If you don't like something, change it. If you can't change it, change your attitude." And, "Courage is the most important of all the virtues, because without courage you can't practice any other virtue consistently. You can practice any virtue erratically, but nothing consistently without courage."

Again with the assistance of Melisha Mitchell, and on January 26, 2012, I went to an address on the south eastside of Chicago looking for my uncle, Ronald Upshaw. The following account is in the words of the woman who answered the door, as I stood on pins and needles as a detective.

"I was talking on the telephone to my neighbor who lives on the second floor. As usual, my mom was sitting in her favorite chair in the front room watching TV and she noticed two middle-aged African-American women coming through the front gate. She thought that they were Jehovah's Witnesses coming to visit the neighbor who is of that faith on the second floor. I was still on the phone with the neighbor and all of a sudden something very strange happened with the doorbells in this three story building in which we all live. The first, second and third floor doorbells rung at once. The doorbells were so loud, and sounded like an out-of-tune horn. I asked my neighbor was she expecting friends to visit her. She replied, "No, not at all." She also said that her doorbell was ringing and she could hear the first and third floor doorbells ringing as well. I told her to hold on and not to hang up."

"So, I went to the intercom system in the hallway area and I pushed "talk" button and said, "WHO IS IT?" A soft voice responded, saying "Jennifer." I am looking for Ronald Upshaw, Sr.

I said, 'PLEASE HOLD ON" it may take a few minutes. I believed she said, "O.K." I thought to myself this is weird. I asked my son Ronald Upshaw, 'who is this woman?' Perhaps, she is a friend of my son. Swiftly, I walked to the front room sun parlor area where my mom was sitting and we looked out the window and saw only one female. We did not recognize this woman dressed in black standing inside the gate of the building. My son was still asleep, so I went to wake him. "Who is Jennifer?" He replied, 'I don't know a Jennifer'. I have to go downstairs to the front entry door to check out this woman who is asking to speak to Ronald Upshaw and that I would call her back as soon as possible."

"I proceeded to the front door and down the steps and I opened the second entry door. I then noticed two females. I was still puzzled by this encounter and contemplating the worst. I was not going to open the first entry door. I was being cautious, so I spoke with the lady who actually rung the doorbells through the glass entry door. Again, I did not see anything unusual, though in my mind I am anticipating something is not quite right. So, I said to her, 'MAY I HELP YOU' or something to that effect."

"The second woman who I did not see out of the window responded saying, 'I am Jennifer' and I am looking for Ronald Upshaw, Senior'. More confused than before, I said to her, 'WHO ARE YOU??? Ronald said he does not know any Jennifer, so who are you and what is this about??? Remember, I would not open the 1st entry, because I was very uncertain as to who these two women were. This Jennifer said, "I need to speak with Ronald Upshaw. It's very important and it's personal."

"Now I thought to myself that I better open this first entry door and find out what this is really all about. I also became worried and a little suspicious about two women coming to talk to a young man. Then Jennifer said to me, I am looking for Ronald Senior, not Junior,

"With tears in her eyes, she held up her hands and said, 'I am just going to trust God. Ronald Upshaw Sr. is my uncle. When I was a baby, my mother Wanda Upshaw gave me up for adoption. Now, I'm looking for my biological family. That's why I need to talk with him'. Now, this took my breath away and I gave her a gentle hug, and said its OK, its OK. Oh, yes, I can see Wanda. She is in you. I see it."

Juanita, my aunt invited Johnnie and I inside her home to further discuss my family, the Upshaws. I met her son (my first cousin Ronald). I immediately saw the resemblance between him and my son. Juanita introduced me to her mother before she suggested that we sit in the kitchen area and talk. She presented me with an obituary of Wanda and Ronald Upshaw Sr. She couldn't believe that a detective wouldn't know that he had been shot and killed in the area of 71st St. and Perry Ave. many years ago. Wanda's obituary in summary reads: Mrs. Wanda N. Jackson was born March 16, 1947, in Chicago, Illinois. In union of William and Ruby Upshaw, who preceded her in death, she leaves her memory to a husband, Charles Jackson, son, Harold Williams. Wanda's remains were entrusted to Burr Oak Cemetery in Alsip, IL. Before Johnnie and I left Juanita's home that afternoon, she assured me that she would place calls to locate my brother (Harold Williams) and a first cousin (Rhonda).

I had gone to over three other Upshaw residences on the south side of Chicago and each proved negative for locating my birth family. Once Johnnie and I went to this fourth Upshaw home, we rang all three bells as I had become accustomed to doing as a detective. After beating around the bush for several minutes with a woman who was most hesitant and suspicious, I finally said, "I'm going to trust God. Wanda Upshaw is my birth mother and I'm looking for my family." The woman looked intently at me for a few seconds and said, "I see it. I see it. I see the Upshaw in you. Wanda had been looking for you, but she didn't know how to find you. She asked me to help her. We didn't know how to find you, but she always said that you would come here. She had hoped I would never change my name from Upshaw." Juanita Upshaw invited us inside of her apartment and she seemed overjoyed and excited about my visit.

Juanita kept her promise to contact my brother and a first cousin who knew Wanda very well. They both asked her, "How did you find her?" She responded, "She found me."

I had asked Johnnie to go with me to the Upshaw residence for a couple of reasons; I wanted moral support and someone to witness the first person I was to meet from my biological family. I couldn't risk forgetting just what was happening to me. Johnnie would be able to affirm that this in fact happened on this date and time. It proved to be a very good decision to have Johnnie there, so I could process this amazing event over and over again throughout the afternoon. She and I shared conversations that afternoon about me having received the strongest lead in finding Juanita since I had started this investigation. The smile on my face lasted beyond the next several hours even though I still had several more unanswered questions.

Before I returned home that day, I received a phone call from a man who identified himself as Harold. I paced the floor followed by standing still in complete awe. I was talking to my brother and he wanted to meet me that evening. "Today!" I thought. "He wants to meet me today!" He picked a McDonald's restaurant between both of our homes for an 8 P.M. meet. When I pulled into the dark parking lot and observed a couple of unoccupied parked cars, there was one car that appeared to have one person seated behind the steering wheel. I entered the restaurant alone. I sat down facing the door. Within seconds, a tall, slightly muscular, medium brown-skinned man walked through the door with a look of certainty that he recognized me and I asked, "Harold?" He nodded and said, "Yeah." I really didn't have to ask because I knew he was my brother. We looked like each other. I stood up and gave him a hug that he without hesitation returned in kind. It honestly felt like I had known him all my life before we even sat down at a table across from one another.

Two hours flew by with my brother at the McDonald's. We exchanged all kinds of information: where we'd lived, what we did, our families and how life had been for the last forty years. We learned that we never lived more than eight miles from each other over all these years and may have unknowingly passed each other. My brother is twenty-two months younger than me and he learned about my adoption when he was about eleven years old. He told me of our brother (Stephen) a year younger than him who died as a baby from SIDS. Stephen's remains are also buried in Burr Oak Cemetery. He especially wanted me to know that our mother grieved my absence from the family for years. She often expressed fits of anger with our maternal grandmother for having to give me away.

We laughed between childhood stories. My eyes watered as he looked at me and said, "It's like a part of Wanda is back." He seemed so happy to see me and able to put a face, a real person, to all the times he had heard about a big sister. When he learned that I was a detective, he smiled and said, "That's what Wanda meant when she said, I'm going to find your big sister and she's going to get you." I laughed at the thought of how right she was without her even knowing me. I could sense that Harold no longer felt alone with my return since many family members had preceded us in death.

As McDonald's prepared to close for the night and they put us out, I walked towards my car, placing a hat on my head. Harold looked at me and said, "Wanda used to wear hats like that." He was referring to the small cap that is sometimes a signature of mine. We laughed and I thought about a line from a book, Synchronicities & Reunion, "I explain our synchronicities by the fact that I always sensed I had a connection to my mother." It was sometime after my meeting with Harold that night when I suggested that he and Juanita join me at Burr Oak Cemetery to visit Wanda and Stephen's grave sites.

At the urging of Melisha Mitchell, I requested Wanda's birth and death certificates from the State of Illinois. The Medical Certificate of Death listed Harold Williams on line 17b as her son and the person of kin that was informed of her death. Harold told me when we met of how he found out about our mother's death. He was called to assist at her home, because she needed medical attention. Upon his arrival, he discovered her being attended to inside of an ambulance outside of the building. It was too late. She was gone. Her health had been declining for a few years.

During January 2012, I re-contacted Curt Holderfield to inform him of Wanda's passing sixteen years earlier. I provided him with her death certificate and requested any other information from my adoption file. He gave me copies of a Family Service Bureau United Charities report dated April 2, 1964 and April 16, 1964. In addition, he supplied me with a document given to my adoptive parents containing known information about me. It was dated July 11, 1966 and the last two of four paragraphs stated the following:

"Bonnie has been born without complications. She has remained in our foster home since she was placed there at the age of four days, and has received excellent attention from the foster parents and the foster family's own children. In April 1965, she had surgery for a herniated navel. She has always seemed a very quick and alert child, very responsive, learns easily, enjoys feeding herself, tries to dress herself, likes to imitate people. Her appetite has always been good, and she is not fond of sweets. She is an amiable and good-natured child, enjoys music." I completely identified with this report in my file over four decades ago as how I feel today. It felt like those paragraphs about me at two years old is the person I am right now (except for not liking sweets)."

On February 18, 2012, Juanita and Harold agreed to accompany me to Burr Oak Cemetery in Alsip, Illinois. We decided to make a day of it by going to lunch afterwards. It was a typical chilly winter day for Chicago, so it called for a warm coat, hat, gloves and a scarf around my neck as the three of us walked through Burr Oak. I had already been warned that a headstone had not yet been purchased for Wanda or anyone in the family except my uncle Ronald Upshaw. Juanita's sister-in-law worked for Burr Oak Cemetery, and she assisted us in finding the exact locations for Wanda and Stephen's burial site. I observed trees bunched together. One of the trees had two large branches from the root. These trees symbolized to me my birth grandfather, grandmother, two uncles and Wanda as the landmark to find the area in the future. I vowed to Harold and myself that I would get a headstone for Wanda within the next twelve months.

Over lunch, Juanita and Harold entertained all of my questions about the Upshaws. I asked about everybody who died much too early: Uncle Ronald first, followed by my grandfather William, grandmother Ruby, and Uncle Billy. I noticed how Harold lovingly referred to Ruby as our grandmother, but I couldn't say it. I preferred saying "Ruby." Juanita politely referred to her as Mrs. Upshaw. I learned that Ronald Sr. had been killed in 1979 at the age of twenty-seven when I was fifteen years old. He had been gunned down in the alley near the family home. Juanita was pregnant with cousin Ronald Jr., who was born that year on December 30th.

Our conversation over lunch was an emotional rollercoaster for me as Harold and Juanita both took turns sharing pieces for me to process about our family. When Harold insisted that Wanda's passing was on her birthday and not March 17th as stated on her death certificate, I thought, Who am I to quarrel about that? I decided to agree with him since he was there. I asked about photos of everybody for the umpteenth time and again I was apologetically told that there were none.

As February approached, plans were in order for a small family reunion on March 18, 2012. I wanted it to center around Wanda's birth date. I set things in motion for a gathering at Leona's restaurant with my brother, my aunt Juanita, my aunt Deborah, cousins, other extended family members and friends. Jean Strauss wanted to videotape this event too, so she arrived in Chicago with her cameras. All this was happening on the same day that the Chicago Tribune decided to release a front-page picture of my brother and I. The prestigious newspaper decided to print the article about five adoptees in Illinois who received their original birth certificates because of the new adoption law. When I read a line from page nine of the early and final editions, I realized that my brother willingly joined me in being open, honest and public about my adoption. The story read: "It blows my mind," said Williams, 46. "Our mother would be so happy. She was trying to find her."

The Javon Watson Experience and Delivery Point Band set up for live music once again and we took over the south side restaurant in style. Cousin Ronald was excited to see Harold's adult sons since Wanda's funeral and it was a long over due family reunion for everybody from the Upshaw bloodline. I met my brother's wife and some of his children for the first time. I immediately saw the resemblance between my birth family and me. I saw myself in the next generation with my nephews. I met some of Harold's childhood friends, and this day would be remembered by me forever. We enjoyed the food, the music and each other as I observed my family grow right before my eyes. My adoptive family was being introduced to my birth family for the first time.

Over the next couple of months, I spent more time with my brother and met more of his immediate family. His oldest son hung out with me one day upon my request. He joined me at a music sound check at a banquet hall. When we were ready to leave, he spotted a young lady going into the building. Jeremiah called to her and told me that she was my niece. She and Jeremiah have different mothers, but have known each other through the years. Jeremiah introduced me to Katrina and all I could think is that if he hadn't been with me that day, I would have passed my beautiful niece and not known that she was my brother's daughter.

Within a short period of time, my cousin Rhonda was able to produce pictures of Wanda and my uncles. My uncle Ronald Upshaw is Rhonda's father and our uncle Billy never had children. He was best remembered as a star basketball player for Simeon in the 1960s. He earned a scholarship to attend college to play ball, but declined the offer. I saw obituaries for everybody except Ruby Upshaw and Billy, better known as "Billy Boy". Rhonda also gave me a picture of our grandmother (Ruby) sitting in a chair smoking a cigarette. When I gazed at Ruby in the picture, I saw myself. I felt hints of my lineage and bloodline from her photograph. I wondered what she would think of my return after four decades when she was the one who insisted that my birth mother place me for adoption. I believe she would be relieved to know that I consider her decision in 1964 to be a good one. After all these years she could have been put at ease. I imagined her asking for my forgiveness, but there was nothing to forgive. I wasn't angry or disappointed in her decision. Everything worked out for me despite what people may say or think about adoption, because that's how I choose to see it. There will always be a need for adoption. There will always be children separated from their birth family. What's important is that an adoptee has a right to know their entire family. We have a right to our original birth certificate.

With all the excitement going on for weeks with my birth family reunion, there was more news during 2012. I quickly learned that the family who lived across the street from where I grew up are related to my brother through marriage. Paulette, who looked out for me during my childhood is my brother's wife's first cousin. I later discovered that my nephews, some of Harold's children spent times across the street, likely when I wasn't too far away. All of this was interesting, to say the least, and I marveled at how things work together.

In August 2012, I searched for my biological father and enlisted the aid of one of my very first partners on the Chicago Police Department. When we first worked together, he was a veteran officer of the force. I heard that my birth father had lived on the far south side in a community called Altgeld Gardens, and my former partner had once lived there too. He was about the same age as my birth mother, and if anyone could help me, he would do it. I knew that Wanda had lived there too. Through him, I soon met with individuals who said that a woman by the name of Lillian could likely further assist me. I was given her phone number and once I placed the call to her, my journey would unfold in the most amazing way.

In the morning hours of a day at work, I called Lillian while sitting alongside Johnnie in a squad car. I told Lillian that I was looking for my birth father. I said, "Your number was given to me by some people who use to live in the Gardens during the 1960s, and you may be able to give me some information."

She was interested in knowing more about why I thought she could help me. I said, "Well, I was adopted and my birth mother's name was Wanda Upshaw. I'm looking for my birth father. Lillian paused and said, "You're Wanda's daughter?" I said, "Yes."

Lillian said, "I can't believe it. Wanda lived two doors from me and my children in the Gardens. I've always known about you being given up for adoption. I was just talking to my homemaker about Wanda, and then you call. You're her daughter?"

Again, I said, "Yes." I asked her could I meet her, and she agreed to see me that day.

Upon meeting Lillian, she hugged me and told me how her two oldest daughters had been Wanda's best friends. She said that they spent a great deal of time together before Wanda's pregnancy in 1964. I thought, "Wow, I found my birth mother's best girlfriends and you tell them things you don't share with anyone else." Lillian was thrilled to see me and wanted to share as much information as she could remember from over forty years ago. She was at least eighty years old, but very clear about the 1960s when her girls and Wanda were teenagers. She said that Wanda had an infectious laugh and a sweet smile. Lillian kept repeating that Wanda never truly forgave her mother for having to give up her baby.

On August 23, 2012, I met Wanda's girlfriends, who were now in their mid-sixties. Raletta and Yolanda greeted me with such warmth and were genuinely glad to make my acquaintance. They shared stories about their relationship with Wanda as teenagers while living in the Gardens. Their mother Lillian was Wanda's godmother and cared for her like a daughter. Raletta described her and Wanda as social butterflies and their boyfriends frequented the Gardens together. Raletta believed my father's name was James "Gibbs" Gilmore. She described him as a "gouster," good-looking and a gentleman. In the sixties, on the South Side of Chicago, the male dress resembling that of the gangsters of the 1930s labeled you as a gouster (pronounced "gawster").

Raletta recalled the time that Wanda went away in the spring of 1964 "We thought she was down South, because the Upshaws went there every year to visit family. We later learned that she went away to have you and never wanted to give up her baby."

Raletta and Yolanda said that they both knew about me all these years and wondered would this day ever come. They were pleased to finally meet Wanda's only daughter. We memorialized the occasion with a photo together and promised to stay in touch. Raletta asked me was I going to look into the information she had given me about Gilmore who she believed to be my birth father. I told her yes.

On November 27, 2012, I spoke with a friend about locating my birth father, but all I knew was the name James Gilmore. I believed he had been born around 1947. I told my friend that Gilmore might have gone to Hirsch High School and he had frequented the Gardens. I added the fact that Gilmore was known as a gouster and had dated Wanda Upshaw when they were teenagers. My friend spoke of a mutual friend born in 1947 who definitely went to Hirsch and likely frequented the Gardens. He too was a gouster. A call was placed to the mutual friend, and we were able to talk over the phone.

He said that he remembered a guy named Gilmore back in the 1960s. They were freshman at the same school and ran the streets together. He said they frequented the Gardens dating girls. They were both gousters. When I explained that I was looking for him, because I believed he was my birth father, he paused and said he would have to call me later. Our conversation ended just like that. A few minutes later, he called me back and said that he didn't want to tell me that the Gilmore that he knew from nearly fifty years ago and fit the description of the person I was looking for died in his twenties. The wind had been let out of my sail, but there was always the hope of DNA testing to find paternal birth family members.

As winter approached again in the Windy City, the headstone for Wanda was completely paid for and ready to be delivered to Burr Oak Cemetery by the end of 2012. It wouldn't be properly placed at her burial site until around April or May in the following year. I selected a rose colored granite with a cross and praying hands on the left side. I asked my brother's opinion and sent him a picture of it. He was pleased with my request to have her headstone read as follows:

My Mother

Wanda N. Upshaw

Williams - Jackson

March 16, 1947-March 16, 1996

I found you.

Harold and I made plans to go see it together on Mother's Day.

Epilogue

Advocates of adoption reform believe all adoptees should be able to possess their original birth certificate. It is an equal right that should be given to all adoptees. In 2010, the state of Illinois changed its adoption law to allow for the opening of this sealed document and thousands of adoptees were granted a long-awaited request. It is the hope of adoption reformists that laws will change to bridge the gap between then and now by granting adoptees access to their first official record of birth.

My birth family and I continue to maintain a harmonious relationship. I am close to my brother and enjoy how similar we are in nature. Through the years, I have come to know nephews, nieces, cousins, great nephews, great nieces and other extended family members since our first meeting. My son has been able to get to know more first cousins and learn that some of them had crossed paths as children. Now, they can readily identify each other as family. I remain in contact with Danny, Ronald, Raletta, and Yolanda. Lillian made her earthly transition in October of 2015. Lastly, I always look forward to spending quality time with my aunt Juanita, because she continues to be a blessing in my life

Journey

It takes a family to touch a community

To reach your destiny

For you and me

When the road gets rough

And the job gets tough

Keep your faith

Through this journey.

Stay focused with perseverance

Think positive

Maintain your endurance

Keep your head up high

Have faith & believe

It's your journey!

-Javon Watson

References

A number of books and other resources were used in the course of writing this book. Some have been directly cited and others have provided valuable information.

Allen, James. As a Man Thinketh. New York: Grosset & Dunlap, 1903.

The 40 Year Secret. Directed by Mary Ann Alton. McNabb Connolly, 2009. Film.

Angelou, Maya. Wouldn't Take Nothing for My Journey Now. New York: Random House, Inc.: 1993

Bailey, Julie Jarrell, and Lynn N. Giddens. The Adoption Reunion Survival Guide: Preparing Yourself for the Search, Reunion, and beyond. Oakland, CA: New Harbinger Publications ; 2001.

Breathnach, Sarah. Simple Abundance: A Daybook of Comfort and Joy. New York: Warner Books, 1995.

Buscaglia, Leo F. Personhood: The Art of Being Fully Human. Thorofare, N.J.: C.B. Slack, 1978.

Campbell, Joseph, and Phil Cousineau. The Hero's Journey: The World of Joseph Campbell: Joseph Campbell on His Life and Work. San Francisco: Harper & Row, 1990.

Carlson, Richard. What about the Big Stuff?: Finding Strength and Moving Forward When the Stakes Are High. New York: Hyperion, 2002.

Chopra, Deepak, and Deepak Chopra. The Seven Spiritual Laws of Success: A Practical Guide to the Fulfillment of Your Dreams. San Rafael, Calif.: Amber-Allen Pub.: 1994.

Cole, Joanna, and Maxie Chambliss. How I Was Adopted: Samantha's Story. New York: Morrow Junior Books, 1995.

Curtis, Jamie Lee, and Laura Cornell. Tell Me Again about the Night I Was Born. New York, NY: Harper Collins, 1996.

DeCosse, Katie, and Jackie Maher. Fifty Years in 13 Days: A Mother/daughter Reunion. Minneapolis, MN: WOW! Publishing Group, 2009.

Dyer, Wayne W. Your Erroneous Zones. New York: Funk & Wagnalls, 1976.

Fessler, Ann. The Girls Who Went Away: The Hidden History of Women Who Surrendered Children for Adoption in the Decades before Roe v. Wade. New York: Penguin Press, 2006.

Ford, Debbie. The Dark Side of the Light Chasers: Reclaiming Your Power, Creativity, Brilliance, and Dreams. New York: Riverhead Books, 1998.

Gibran, Kahlil. The Prophet. New York: Knopf, 1952.

Gilmarten, Kevin M. Emotional Survival for Law Enforcement: A Guide for Officers and Their Families. Arizona: E-S Press, 2002.

The Blind Side. Directed by John Lee Hancock. Warner Home Video, 2010. Film.

Hicks, Esther. The Law of Attraction: The Basics of the Teachings of Abraham. Carlsbad, Calif.: Hay House, 2006.

Secrets & Lies. Directed by Mike Leigh. CBS Fox Video/Twentieth Century Fox Home Entertainment, 1997. Film.

Lifton, Betty Jean. Twice Born: Memoirs of an Adopted Daughter. New York: McGraw Hill, 1975.

Losier, Michael J. Law of Attraction: The Science of Attracting More of What You Want and Less of What You Don't. New York: Wellness Central, 2007.

March, Karen Ruth. The Stranger Who Bore Me: Adoptee-birth Mother Relationships. Toronto: University of Toronto Press, 1995.

McClausand, Children of Circumstance. Chicago, IL: R.R. Donnelly & Sons Company, 1976.

McMahon, Patrick. Becoming Patrick: A Memoir. San Diego, Calif.: Deep Root Press, 2011.

Meyer, Joyce. Enjoying Where You Are on the Way to Where You Are Going: Learning How to Live a Joyful Spirit-led Life. New York: Warner Books, 2002.

Miller, Kathryn Ann, and Jami Moffett. Did My First Mother Love Me?: A Story for an Adopted Child : With a Special Section for Adoptive Parents. Buena Park, Calif.: Morning Glory Press, 1994.

Nydam, Ronald J. Adoptees Come of Age Living within Two Families. Louisville, Ky.: Westminster John Knox Press, 1999.

Patterson, Eleanora, and Barbara Ernst Prey. Twice-upon-a-time: Born and Adopted. Brattleboro, VT: EP Press, 1987.

Peacock, Carol Antoinette, and Shawn Costello Brownell. Mommy Far, Mommy Near: An Adoption Story. Morton Grove, Ill.: Albert Whitman, 2000.

Peale, Norman Vincent. The Power of Positive Living. New York: Doubleday, 1990.

Pertman, Adam. Adoption Nation: How the Adoption Revolution Is Transforming Our Families-- and America. 2nd ed. Boston, Mass.: Harvard Common Press, 2011.

Richmond, Marianne R. I Wished for You: An Adoption Story. Minneapolis, Minn.: Marianne Richmond Studios, 2008.

Richardson, Cheryl. Take Time for Your Life: A Personal Coach's Seven-step Program for Creating the Life You Want. New York: Broadway Books, 1998.

Robinson, Evelyn. Adoption Reunion. Christies Beach, South Australia: Clova Publications, 2009.

Mother and Child. Directed by Rodrigo A. Sony Pictures Home Entertainment, 2010. Film.

Rogers, Fred, and Jim Judkis. Let's Talk about It: Adoption. New York, NY: Putnam & Grosset Group, 1994.

Ruiz, Don Miguel. The Four Agreements: A Practical Guide to Personal Freedom. San Rafael, Calif.: Amber-Allen Pub. : 1997.

Smalley, Betsy Keefer, and Jayne E. Schooler. Telling the Truth to Your Adopted or Foster Child: Making Sense of the past. Westport, Conn.: Bergin & Garvey, 2000.

Sorosky, Arthur D., and Annette Baran. The Adoption Triangle: The Effects of the Sealed Record on Adoptees, Birth Parents, and Adoptive Parents. Garden City, N.Y.: Anchor Press, 1978.

Stiffler, LaVonne Harper. Synchronicity and Reunion: The Genetic Connection of Adoptees and Birthparents. Hobe Sound, Fla.: FEA Pub., 1992.

Strauss, Jean A. S. Beneath a Tall Tree: A Story about Us. Claremont, Calif.: Areté Publishing, 2001.

A Simple Piece of Paper. Directed by Jean Strauss. Film.

Tolle, Eckhart. A New Earth: Awakening to Your Life's Purpose, New York: Plume, 2006.

Tolle, Eckhart. The Power of Now: A Guide to Spiritual Enlightenment. Novato, Calif.: New World Library, 1999.

Vanzant, Iyanla. In the Meantime--: Finding Yourself and the Love That You Want. New York, NY: Simon & Schuster, 1998.

Verrier, Nancy Newton. The Primal Wound: Understanding the Adopted Child. Baltimore: Gateway Press, 1993.

Walvoord, Linda, and Judith Friedman. Adoption Is for Always. Niles, Ill.: A. Whitman, 1986.

Warshaw, Melinda A. A Legitimate Life. Self published, 2012.

Wetzstein, Cheryl. "All States Urged to Give Adult Adoptees Their History; Birth Parents Should Decide, Opposition Says." The Washington Times, July 16, 2010. Accessed October 9, 2015. http://www.highbeam.com

Zinn, Jon. Wherever You Go, There You Are: Mindfulness Meditation in Everyday Life. New York: Hyperion, 1994.

Zukav, Gary. The Seat of the Soul. New York, NY: Rockefeller Center, 1989.

Jennifer and son Andre

Harold and Jennifer
"My big sister means the world to me formed in a bond of distance pulled back together by fate and built from a mother who never forgot and would never let me forget. She shared a love for us both and we both share an undying love for her and each other. I LOVE YOU SIS!!!

Jennifer's birth mother Wanda

Jennifer's Mom & Dad

ABOUT THE AUTHOR

Jennifer Dyan Ghoston began her study of the social sciences at the University of Illinois at Chicago prior to joining the Chicago Police Department as a sworn officer in 1987. She later received an undergraduate BA degree in Criminal/Social Justice from Lewis University/Romeoville, IL. And in 2003, she earned an MBA from St. Xavier University/Chicago, IL with a concentration in Training and Performance Management.

It is her desire to always join in the effort to bridge the gap between our communities and law enforcement. Most importantly, she is passionate about her commitment to adoption reform along with other adoptees, birth and adoptive parents.

Contact information as follows:

Email: JenniferDyan@aol.com

Write it on your heart that everyday is the best day in the year.

He is rich who owns the day.

And no one owns the day who allows it to be invaded with fret and anxiety.

Finish each day and be done with it.

You've done what you could.

Some blunders and absurdities no doubt crept in.

Forget them as soon as you can.

Tomorrow is a new day.

Begin it well and serenely with too high of a spirit to be encumbered with your old nonsense.

This new day is too dear with its hopes and invitations to waste a moment on the yesterdays.

-Ralph Waldo Emerson

Made in the USA
Lexington, KY
20 November 2016